AWAKENED FROM WITHIN

AWAKENED FROM WITHIN:

Meditations on the Christian Life

Brother Roger of Taizé

Doubleday & Company, Inc., Garden City, New York
1987

Library of Congress Cataloging-in-Publication Data
Roger, frère, 1915–
Awakened from within.

1. Spiritual life—Reformed authors. 2. Reconciliation—Religious aspects—Christianity. 3. Christian
union. I. Title.
BV4501.2.R625 1987   248.4   86-19615
ISBN 0-385-23536-4

Copyright © 1987 by Brother Roger of Taizé

Acknowledgments

Material in the chapters "The Silence of Contemplation," "That Unique Communion Called the Church," "Go to Meet Those Who Cannot Believe," "Letter to Religious Communities," "All or Nothing," "Avoid Separating the Generations," and "People of Peace" is from *Afire with Love: Meditations on Peace and Unity* by Brother Roger of Taizé (Copyright © 1981 by Les Presses de Taizé; reprinted by permission of The Crossroad Publishing Company).

Material in the chapters "The Essential Hidden from Our Eyes," "From Doubt Toward Believing," and "Hope That Invents the World Anew" is from *A Life We Never Dared Hope For* (Copyright © 1981 by Les Presses de Taizé; published in the United States by Winston Press); and "Aflame with Christ's Love" from *Living Today for God* (published in the United States by Winston Press; copyright © 1980 by Les Presses de Taizé). These are reprinted here by special arrangement with A. R. Mowbray.

The following material from books by A. R. Mowbray is reprinted with permission of the publisher: "The Rule of Taizé," "Celebrate the Moment with God," "Happy Are They Who Die for Love," "The Wonder of a Love," "Accompany Christ by a Simple Life," "A Life We Never Dared Hope For," and "Struggle with a Reconciled Heart" from *Parable of Community* (English language edition published in 1980 by A. R. Mowbray; copyright © 1980, 1984 by Les Presses de Taizé); "Preface," "A Way Out of a Dead End," and "Leaven of Hope in the World" from *A Heart That Trusts* (Copyright © 1986 by Les Presses de Taizé); "The Silence of Contemplation," "A Way Out of a Dead End," and "Struggle and Contemplation" from *Struggle and Contemplation* (Revised Edition, copyright © 1983 by Les Presses de Taizé); "In Everyone, a Unique Gift," "Reawakened from Within," "Taking Risks for World Peace," "From Doubt to a Fine Human Hope," and "Witness to a Different Future" from *And Your Deserts Shall Flower* (first published in English in 1984 by A. R. Mowbray, copyright © 1983 by Les Presses de Taizé); and "Following You, O Christ" (Prayers) from *Praying Together* (published in English by A. R. Mowbray, copyright © 1981, 1985 by Les Presses de Taizé).

All other material, including Letters, is reprinted with permission of the Taizé community.

CONTENTS

PREFACE

Faced with the urgent need for the Gospel to be made present at the heart of the human family, we are conscious of how limited the resources of our community are when compared with the vast horizons opening out on this eve of a new millennium.

What are you, little community? An efficient instrument?

No. Never. Fine as that may be.

Perhaps a group of men united to be stronger, humanly speaking, in order to realize their own aims?

Not that either.

So could we be living a common life in order to be comfortable together?

No. The community would then become an end in itself, and that would allow us to settle down in cosy little nests. Being happy together? Certainly, but in the context of the offering of our lives.

What are you, little community, spread out in different parts of the world?

A parable of communion, a simple reflection of that unique communion which is the Body of Christ, his Church, and therefore a ferment in the human family.

What is your calling?

In our common life, we can only move forward by discovering ever anew the miracle of love, in daily forgiveness, heartfelt trust and peace-filled contemplation of those entrusted to us. When we move away from the miracle of love all is lost, everything comes apart.

Little community, what might be God's desire for you?

To be made alive by drawing nearer to the holiness of Christ.

INTRODUCTION:

A CONVERSATION WITH
BROTHER ROGER OF TAIZÉ

The ecumenical community of Taizé began in 1940, when a young man named Roger, the son of a Swiss father and a French mother, came and settled in the tiny village of Taizé, in the Burgundy region of eastern France. It was wartime, and he chose Taizé because it enabled him to help political refugees, primarily Jews, to escape from occupied France. After living alone for three years, he was joined by three others, and together they began living a life of prayer, work and hospitality for the sake of Christ and the Gospel.

In coming to Taizé, Brother Roger's intention was not to start a new church or denomination but to form a "parable of community," a sign of reconciliation rooted in the monastic tradition, to gather together men who would make a life commitment to celibacy and to material and spiritual sharing. Today, the community includes over eighty brothers from some twenty different countries. They are Catholic, as well as from Anglican, Lutheran and Reformed origins. Since 1966, members of a Catholic international community of sisters who live according to the spirit of St. Ignatius of Loyola have settled in a nearby village; they collaborate with the brothers in Taizé and elsewhere.

Not all of the brothers are permanently in Taizé. A part of the community lives in small groups throughout the world, in poor areas of Africa, Asia and Latin America as well as in Manhattan's "Hell's Kitchen," where they live, work and pray in the midst of tensions and divisions. Brother Roger himself has spent part of each year living among the poor and forgotten, and visiting Church leaders, including the last few Popes, to search with them for concrete steps to reconciliation.

Beginning in the 1960s, tens of thousands of people, primarily young adults, have come to Taizé in their searching. During the week-long meetings run by the Community throughout the year, they explore the sources of faith. Regularly, large gatherings bring together many in the churches of Europe, North America and other continents. But Taizé has always refused to create its own movement, placing instead the accent on becoming involved in one's own particular situation, in the local church.

Recently, Brother Roger responded to the following questions.

Brother Roger, what motivated you to start an ecumenical community?

Now that I am old, I realize that it began in my earliest childhood. One of the biggest shocks in my life occurred, I think, at that time, at the end of World War I, when my maternal grandmother, a remarkable woman, arrived from France to live with us.

My parents admired her. Why? Because she was a woman of courage. Her three sons were at the front. She was a widow. She lived in the north of France. Even when the shells were falling round her home she would not leave. She wanted to keep on giving shelter to refugees—old people, children, pregnant women. She didn't leave until the very last minute, when there was really no other possibility. She then left for the south.

She was one of those who longed for the time when no one would ever again have to experience what she had gone through. For this to happen, Christians would have to become reconciled; that was the first thing to be done. Christians in Europe were killing one another. Let them at least be reconciled and so avoid another war. That, she told us, was her bequest to us, her spiritual testament.

She came of old Protestant stock (in the house where my mother was born, there was a tower with a secret room where the pastor was hidden in times of persecution). But in order to make reconciliation a reality in her own heart without delay, she went into a Catholic church to pray. It was as if she had sensed that the Eucharist in the Catholic Church was a source of unanimity for the faith. The miracle of her life was that, in reconciling within her those two origins, she managed to avoid becoming a symbol of repudiation of her own people.

What struck you most about her life?

For one thing, that she had the courage to share the lot of those who were suffering most. And on the other hand, I realized that in going to pray in the Catholic church she had made a gesture which took just as much courage as taking in refugees. This insight of hers made a deep impression on me: My whole life has been marked by it. While I was still a child, it gave me a catholic soul. I have continued along the road opened up by that old woman. Following in the footsteps of my grandmother I found my own identity, without becoming a symbol of repudiation for anyone, by reconciling in the depths of my heart the current of faith of my Protestant origins with the faith of the Catholic Church.

Can it be said that concern for the poor was just as important as ecumenism at the beginning of Taizé's existence?

Certainly. In 1940, at the beginning of the Second World War, when I settled alone in Taizé, I realized how urgent it was to offer hospitality to political refugees fleeing from the Nazi persecution and needing to be hidden and helped to escape. In doing that I was certainly making a gesture identical to her own.

What role did prayer play at that time in your life?

When I was young, I didn't dare to pray "out of intellectual honesty," to use the expression I favored at that time. I didn't really lose my faith, in the sense of experiencing deep unbelief. I still had confidence in people who had an intuition of God, but I was not able myself to have the same intuition. I had confidence in my grandmother, and I thought: Certainly that essential reality, which is Christ, to which she constantly turns, must exist—I can't deny it because her life was based on it. But I couldn't really see how to encounter Christ myself. And the major obstacle was the divisions between Christians.

Afterwards there was a succession of stages. After the period when I didn't dare to pray, the day came when I was able to say a few words to God. I didn't pray for myself, but for the healing of someone in my family whom I loved. I knelt at the foot of my bed, and all I could say was the words of a Psalm in the translation used then: "Thy voice in my heart says, seek my face. Thy face, Lord, do I seek" (Psalm 27).

Then I became firmly convinced that, if I wanted to accomplish anything that would last, it was essential to discover a few basic guidelines to refer to throughout my life, a foundation on which to build. I was about eighteen when I became convinced that a person cannot develop his character and acquire inner unity unless he chooses a few guidelines. Nothing lasting can be built without some basic reference points to return to our whole life long.

Those points of reference made up our original Rule, and they recur throughout what we now call "the sources of Taizé." In particular: throughout your day let work and rest be quickened by the word of God; be filled with the spirit of the Beatitudes: joy, simplicity, mercy.

So in writing that original Rule, and then in developing it in the Rule of Taizé, you wanted to reintroduce monastic life within the Reformation churches?

I have never wanted to be part of a process of "restoring" the monastic life. I have never believed in such a process. Nor did I ever want simply to integrate monastic life into the churches of the Reformation alone: that would have merely consolidated the parallelism between denominations which blocks communion among Christians to such an extent. What I have always been passionately seeking, I believe, is something very concrete: a parable of communion incarnate in the lives of a few men, for words have no credibility unless they are lived out. I was haunted by the idea: Why not, by our lives, put into the dough of the divided churches, all the churches, a yeast of communion?

What are the essentials of an ecumenical community?

Very soon after I first arrived in Taizé, I knew that it would be possible to create a monastic "order," a "congregation." But I always refused to, right from the start. It would have been too unwieldy. A small community, on the other hand, is able to adapt constantly to developments in human society, and society is developing more rapidly today than ever before. The most important thing is the sign-value of a community. Making it concrete. This always kept coming up: make it concrete; don't get lost in too many abstract ideas. That's where the man of the soil in me comes to the fore.

A Christian awakens others to God, above all, by the life he or she leads. In the same way, a community awakens others to the meaning of communion and creates ferments of communion more by its life than by its words. Words only become credible when they are lived out. Words are necessary, but they come afterwards, to express something that is already being lived out.

Is a life of prayer another of the strong points?

It is an immense reservoir utterly beyond our comprehension. Our own words only enter into it as a very poor prayer. And that is just as true for me now, at my age, as it was when at the age of twenty-five I arrived in Taizé. It's true that the light of a presence can sometimes flash through our prayer, and for that presence no words are adequate. Nevertheless, essentially prayer is always poverty-stricken.

Your first years in Taizé must have been extremely difficult.

How could it have been otherwise? It was wartime. I was alone and inexperienced. Hiding political refugees, dealing with the inevitable questions, was not easy. But I think I knew how to cope with my suffering. I would sing for hours at a time while I worked, and it seemed to me joy could be found there: in singing a great deal, and praying three times a day.

Right away I learned to work with my hands. I learned, for instance, that a cow will give more milk if she is milked three times a day instead of twice. From the very beginning, and still today, we never accepted any donations or inheritances. We have always worked for our living. That is because we don't want to be materially dependent on anybody. This refusal to accept gifts, even inheritances from our families, has certainly taught us a lot about sharing. And that makes life more intense. It is also creative, because it requires us to think about the needs of everyday life and to keep our feet firmly planted on the ground.

I said to myself: the more someone wants to live in response to the absolute of God's call, the more essential it is to insert that absolute into human suffering—to test the authenticity of a spiritual experience by confronting it with suffering humanity. When I was living alone with the political refugees, I had set up a small oratory in the house. I prayed there, morning, noon and evening, just as we do today. When some of the refugees wished to pray with me, I didn't want them to. I was afraid they might feel under an obligation, because I had shown them hospitality. I was afraid the hospitality had put pressure on their freedom of choice. I know that one or two of them suffered from my refusal; they prayed in their rooms. I thought that if they felt bound to join me it

would not be honest, it would not be fair. Those two words played a
large role in the consciousness of my family.

Can you tell me why you were so attached to Pope John XXIII?

I had a meeting with him once a year. Through him I was able to
understand all the dimensions of the Church which the human mind
does not even suspect. Pope John could have spoken to us in the language of tradition. But instead his words went so far, they were so
powerful, that even today, at every difficult moment, they urge me on.

It seemed to me that in that aged man there were accents of prophecy. He had insights, presentiments of the future of the Church. But it
was a good thing that he was not conscious of it, so that he remained
what he was, a normal human being, laughing and weeping. Sometimes
tears came to his eyes. For me he was a kind of icon of the Christians of
northern Italy.

*Sometimes people compare you with St. Francis of Assisi. What do you think
about that?*

It is something that would never even occur to me. When people say
exaggerated things to me, I change the subject. When I am thanked for
the spirit of Taizé, I reply that there is no spirit of Taizé. Then some
people ask me for autographs or other nonsense of that sort. I tell them
that a Christian cannot agree with expressions focusing on himself and
not on the one Reality that matters. I am a humble servant and I will
remain so until my dying day.

What does being prior mean to you?

During one of our community's council meetings, I reminded my
brothers that from the very beginning I have always refused the title of
prior inside the community. I am their brother. I am only the poor
servant of community. And in recent years we have noticed that, even
for the outside world, the title "prior" is necessary only very rarely, to
describe rapidly a ministry. To be shown special consideration because
of a church title is not in the spirit of the Gospel. And sometimes I state
clearly why I reject what has so often wrought havoc in the churches:
the seeking of prestige and honor through ecclesiastical office.

It is not possible for church leaders to add honorific titles to their
service of God. It is no longer possible to accept that an honor be
attached to a pastoral ministry.

How do you see Taizé?

As a parable of communion open to the universal. A parable lived in the lives of brothers of different origins, Catholic and non-Catholic. Nothing but a parable to advance towards that unique communion called the Church. A number of times during our existence as a community, people have tried to talk us into starting a new Church. We could have done so, but such an undertaking would have contradicted our search for communion, our passion for the Church and for the ecumenical vocation. It would have made us part of that well-known process which in past centuries has fragmented the Body of Christ. We have suffered too much from that process to use it ourselves.

There is no "Taizé spirituality." All we are interested in is being a part of the prayer of the Church of the ages. In the same way, we are careful not to let a "Taizé movement" begin among young people, a movement that ultimately would attach itself to our community. The important thing for us is to exercise together with the young a pastoral activity of reconciliation in the churches. The decision to encourage people to enter into the life of parishes and congregations, where all the ages are present, is significant in this respect. Amidst the upheavals of modern-day society, parishes, no matter how fragile they may sometimes be, remain all over the world places of continuity able to withstand the successive crises and to be centers of local reconciliation.

The age-old process that consists in starting a new church every time there is a crisis goes against the catholicity of the Church and makes reconciliation impossible.

Are your relations with the Protestant churches good?

In the 1950s, some Protestant church leaders could not accept the idea of lifelong commitments—it was in such contradiction to more than four centuries of Reformation history. Today they understand, and I think that, generally speaking, we inspire their trust.

Do you think that a reconciliation among Christians is possible?

What captivates us most is the reconciliation of the whole human family. If Christians are looking for reconciliation, that is not in order to become stronger against others, it is in order to stand together as a ferment of peace in the very places where the human family is being torn apart. When they are reconciled, even just a few of them, Christians can reverse the determinisms of hatred and war and give renewed human hope to those who are overcome by passivity, discouragement and a life without meaning.

Concerning the reconciliation of Christians, at the beginning of the Second Vatican Council it was believed that reconciliation would come about among church institutions, and that this would happen chiefly through those in charge of these institutions. We have to admit that this reconciliation did not happen. There is no point in vain regrets: it was an impossibility. As if those in charge were restrained by past history to such an extent that they could not take the step of reconciliation, which would require decades.

Just look at the whole relationship between Pope Paul VI and Patriarch Athenagoras. Both wanted to concelebrate. Athenagoras could not. He was kept back. The situation was painful for both men. But God never brings us to a standstill: since we have not yet arrived at the goal we hoped for, it means that God is asking us to look for even simpler and more concrete ways. Perhaps we had projected a human desire, with insufficient insight into situations. Many people can accept that those in charge of Christian confessions need time to resolve the structural questions raised by ecumenism. They can understand that there is a need for ecumenical agencies which move with their own characteristic perseverance. But then, what concrete way can be proposed to turn into an immediate reality the reconciliation that denominational institutions are not able to accomplish?

I have come to this conclusion: the ecumenical institutions may indeed need a great deal of time to make reconciliation a reality, but here and now, in the present period of transition, all non-Catholics can reconcile within themselves the faith of their family of origin with the faith of the Catholic Church.

Today, I can discern no other way to permit non-Catholics to become reconciled with the Catholic Church without anybody being humiliated in the process—and that is of the utmost importance at the present time. With this in mind, a gesture towards the baptized of non-Catholic origin is necessary from the authority of the Catholic Church. It is more essential than ever before not to cut off any human being from the best of his or her roots. Christ Himself did not want to destroy the best of his people's inheritance, the Law and the prophets; he wanted to fulfill them. In a period of history when family ties and the bonds between the generations are under strain, who would not do the utmost to bring about reconciliation without wounding the souls of members of one's own family of origin?

Concretely, how can this be done?

With reconciliation in mind, it is an illusion to think that each can have all. When two estranged people seek reconciliation, it is essential first of all for each of them to discover the special gifts the other has. If each asserts that he or she already has all the gifts and wants to bring everything and receive nothing, reconciliation will never come about.

It is just the same with the separated churches. Reconciliation can never mean the victory of some and the humiliation of the rest. It is built on the discovery of the gifts placed in others; it cannot tolerate some having to reject those from whom they received their faith in Christ. The discovery of the gifts of others cannot lead anybody to be a symbol of rejection.

With concrete reconciliation in mind, will we be able to pass through a period in which we place the greatest emphasis on the specific gifts of each tradition, without wasting a single moment in confrontation and without trying to find out who was wrong and who was right?

You speak of specific gifts. In this respect, how do you see Protestantism?

Their own particular gift is to be first and foremost the churches of the Word. The Catholic Church, too, has always tried to find in Scripture a source for living in God. But one of the constants flowing through the history of the Protestant churches has always been this: as soon as a word from God has been understood (not a word taken in isolation, of course, but set in the whole context of the Scriptures), it has an impact on a person's life.

If we remember the quality of the great Protestant divines of the seventeenth and eighteenth centuries, whose writings and poems were transposed with rare intensity into chorales and hymns by Johann Sebastian Bach, for example, then we can understand better how the Word of God was loved and taken seriously in the life of the individual, to what extent it inspired an inner life, how it influenced and stirred Protestant Christians to the very core of their being. Isn't that the best of Protestantism?

And the Catholic Church?

The Catholic Church is above all the Church of the Eucharist; her specific gift lies there. Through storm and stress she has allowed the Eucharist to remain a source of unanimity of the faith, like an underground river flowing through her entire history, even the darkest periods.

The Eucharist, presence of Christ worshiped in the bread and wine, cannot be received as a routine, but always in a spirit of reconciliation and repentance, simply, like a child. And this is true for us until the autumn of our years. When, at the beginning of this century, Pope Pius X opened the Eucharist to little children, he showed rare intuition.

Remaining before the Eucharist in deep inner silence, even when nothing seems to be happening, many have matured the great decisions of their lives. They let themselves be penetrated down to the very depths of their being, to what is called the unconscious. "My Kingdom is within you"—though we may not necessarily feel any resonance within our hearts, the Eucharist makes these words of Christ a reality here and now, even for those who hardly dare imagine such a thing.

The Catholic Church, first and foremost the Church of the Eucharist, has another particular gift. She has set apart men to bring forgiveness, to unbind on earth what is then instantly unbound in the Kingdom, to remove the burden weighing too heavily on people's shoulders, to wipe out even the immediate past.

In confession, there is an opportunity to express in the most spontaneous way possible what weighs upon our conscience. To tell everything about our faults is something no one can manage. But to say what comes to mind at the moment is already tremendous—it enables us to receive in the sacrament the unimaginable forgiveness of God.

Nowadays some have thought it was necessary to play down sin, or even to deny its existence, in order to liberate people from their guilt. In fact, it cannot be denied that, far from freeing from guilt, this attitude diffuses the guilt throughout the personality and spreads it out to the point where it cannot be reached, let alone be uprooted.

Some people, with great seriousness, make frequent use of confession. For them it is so necessary to live from this visible sign that wipes out all the past. Others, just as seriously, go less often; they are so aware that God keeps them in his forgiveness.

In both cases confession, however clumsy, is essential, so that we can experience anew the freshness of the Gospel, and undergo a rebirth. By it we learn to blow remorse itself away, like a child blowing away a fallen leaf. That is God's happiness, the dawning of perfect joy.

And finally, what would you say about the Orthodox churches?

The Orthodox churches, which have the same vision of the Eucharist and the ministry as the Catholic Church, have brought the Risen Christ so close to daily life throughout their history. They have done this particularly through the prayer of the Church, to such an extent that even non-believers can sense in the Orthodox liturgy the ineffable presence of the living God.

Why are young people throughout the world so attracted to Taizé? And why is Taizé so interested in youth?

When I was young, I was surprised that young people were made to keep a certain distance from their elders. I respected that distance; I do not think that I suffered from it, but it astonished me. At that time, when there were so many divisions among people, I kept on asking myself, Why these antagonisms, this inability to understand one another? And I wondered: Does there exist, here on earth, a way to understand everything in another person?

Then came a day—I can still remember the date, and I could describe the place: the subdued light of a late summer evening, darkness settling over the countryside—a day when I made a resolution. I said to myself: If such a way exists, begin with yourself and commit yourself to understanding everything in every human being; become the man who can understand everything. That day, I knew the resolve I had made was final and would last until I died. It consisted simply in returning again and again during my entire lifetime to that once-and-for-all resolution: Seek to understand instead of seeking to be understood.

I constantly say to myself, when every day after the common prayer I stay on in our church to listen to the young: When I was young, in my heart of hearts I wanted to be listened to like this. Why are they suffering? What lies beneath their hearts? What has tied them up in knots? What are their inner prisons? And then immediately another question arises, one that is more vital: What are each one's special gifts? How can we help them to discover them? That is the most important thing. Everything else, the past, even the moment which has just gone by, is already drowned with Christ in the water of baptism.

Pope John XXIII tried to discover the "signs of the times" in the world of today. Personally, what signs do you see in today's youth?

Since the 1970s we have noticed aspirations and difficulties they all have in common. Everywhere young people (not all young people, of course) are seeking God, often after apparently having given up all reference to him. This aspiration is found in the southern continents as well as in the north. On this quest, those who are not sidetracked and who persevere find that they develop deep roots. And that is marvelous.

There are also the troubles of our time—the age of disillusionment, the great void of which many are conscious. Once they had hope, splendid human hope in a just society. But it has to be admitted that what was hoped for most has not come about; the evolution of human society has turned out otherwise than many had desired. So now there is disappointment and often discouragement. Discouragement is deadly. It leads people to withdraw into groups of just a few like-minded individuals. They turn in on themselves and try to find contentment all by themselves. The meaning of life matters little. That is one effect of the agonizing discouragement felt by youth today.

We have two attitudes to deal with, to simplify things a bit: a tremendous aspiration to persevere in seeking God and at the same time deep disillusionment at the failure of splendid human hopes.

But there is also tremendous hope for peace in the world presently arising among young Christians and some of their elders. Their hope makes it possible for the Church, even in her present tribulation, to live in a deep-rooted confidence and to try to communicate a taste for the living God. These young people know that, to follow Christ, they are called to fight not with weapons of power, but with reconciled hearts. They seek to share, knowing that world peace depends in part on more equitable sharing among all peoples.

Everywhere, little awakenings are taking place, small groups springing up. If these small communities place the leaven of the Gospel in the dough of old parishes so often fearful for their future, then the hardened crust of the old parishes will crack. When these small groups, instead of running away, remain within, unsuspected creative forces come to life. They are overturning the ramparts of rigidity.

What message do you have for Americans who are searching for a spiritual life?

If they could see that the greatest mystery, the most profound and generous of all, is the Risen Christ present for every human being without exception, then maybe they would understand why the main thing in our life is our friendship with Christ, our confidence in him. Because he is risen, he is present for all. Whether they recognize him or not, he suffers with all who suffer, he weeps with all who weep, he goes through agony with all in agony, he rejoices with all who rejoice. When we glimpse this reality, then welcoming Christ into our life becomes the one thing that really matters.

ONE

THE RULE OF TAIZÉ

Foreword

Brother, if you consent to a common rule, you can only do so on account of Christ and the Gospel.

From now on, your worship and your service are integrated in a brotherly community, itself set in the body of the Church. In the inner searching so necessary for your Christian life, you are stimulated by others' dynamism. You are not alone anymore. Your brothers are to be reckoned with in everything.

So, far from groaning under the burden of a rule, rejoice: refusing to look back, borne along with all by one and the same Word, every day you can once again hasten on toward Christ.

These pages contain the minimum needed for a community to grow up in Christ and devote itself to a common service of God. There is a risk implied in this resolve to set down only the essentials: your freedom might become a pretext for living according to your own impulses.

The sole grace of our Lord Jesus Christ assures you of salvation, so you have no disciplines to observe for their own sakes. The one aim of your search for self-mastery is greater availability. No pointless abstaining, keep to what God commands. Bear the burdens of others,

accept whatever hurts each day brings, so that you are concretely in
communion with the sufferings of Christ: there lies our main discipline.

You are afraid that a common rule may stifle your personality when
its purpose is to free you from useless fetters, the better to bear responsibility and exercise all the boldness possible in your ministry.

You would restrict your understanding of the Gospel if you withheld
some part of yourself for fear of losing your life. Unless the grain of
wheat dies, you cannot hope to see your life grow up and blossom into
the fullness of Christian living.

Never stand still, advance with your brothers, race toward the goal in
the steps of Christ. His path is a way of light—I am, but also, you are
the light of the world . . . For the light of Christ to penetrate you, it is
not enough to contemplate it (as though you were purely spirit); you
have set out resolutely, body and soul, along that path.

Be a sign for others of joy and brotherly love.

Open yourself to all that is human and you will find that every vain
desire to escape from the world disappears. Be present to your age;
adapt yourself to the conditions of the moment. Father, I pray you, not
to take them out of the world, but to keep them from evil.

Love the deprived, all who are suffering from injustice and thirsting
for justice. Jesus had special concern for them. Never be afraid of their
bothering you.

To your parents, show deep affection; let its very quality help them to
recognize the absolute nature of your vocation.

Love your neighbor, whatever his religious or ideological point of
view.

Never resign yourself to the scandal of the separation of Christians,
all so readily professing love for their neighbor, yet remaining divided.
Make the unity of Christ's Body your passionate concern.

Common Prayer

THE DISCIPLES, full of great joy, met in the temple praising you, and I too will tell all the wonders you have done; you have turned my mourning into gladness, you have girded me with joy, so my heart will sing your praise and not keep silent.

Our common prayer is set within the communion of saints; but for this communion with the believers of every age to become a reality, we have to give ourselves to fervent intercession for humanity and the Church.

The Lord could do without our intercessions and our praise. Yet it is God's mystery that he demands of us, his fellow workers, to keep on praying and never tire.

Let us be careful to seek the inner meaning of liturgical actions and strive to perceive, in signs accessible to people of flesh and blood, an invisible reality pertaining to the Kingdom. But let us beware of multiplying these signs, being careful to preserve their simplicity—the token of their worth for the Gospel.

The liturgical vestment is worn to remind us that our whole being has been clothed by Christ. It is a way of expressing our praise of the Lord other than by words.

The praise of Christ expressed by the liturgy penetrates us insofar as it continues throughout the humblest tasks. In the regular rhythm of our common prayer, the love of Jesus grows in us, we do not know how.

Common prayer does not dispense us from personal prayer. The one sustains the other. Let us take time each day to renew our personal intimacy with Jesus Christ.

In Christ's company we are filled beyond measure; therefore let us surrender ourselves to the living Word of God, allowing it to reach the secret depths of our being and take possession not only of our minds but of our bodies as well.

Christ, the Word made flesh, gives himself to us visibly in the Sacrament. Draw strength from the Eucharist, the meal of thanksgiving, and never forget that it is offered to the sick among the people of God. It is for you, frail and weak as you always are.

There is no point in being upset during the common prayer if the brothers find it hard to keep together while singing. Certainly, the surrender of ourselves to a life hidden in Christ can never justify laziness or routine; it can only signify the active participation of our whole being, mind and body together.

If your attention wanders, return to prayer as soon as you realize the fact, without lamenting over it. Should you experience your weakness even in the very heart of the prayer, do not forget that in you the essential has already been accomplished.

There are days when the common prayer becomes a burden to you. Then simply offer your body; your presence is already proof of your desire, not realizable for the moment, to praise your Lord. Believe in Christ's presence within you, even if you can feel no apparent resonance.

Meals

EVERY MEAL OUGHT to be an agape overflowing with brotherly love, joy and simplicity of heart.

The silence sometimes observed during a meal offers refreshment when you are tired, or communion in prayer for the companion who is sharing bread with you.

The Council

THE AIM OF the council is to seek all the light possible on the will of Christ for the ongoing life of the community. The first step is to bring yourself into silence, to be ready to listen to your Lord.

Nothing is more unfavorable to objective judgment than the ties of particular affinity; we may incline to support a brother in the perhaps unconscious hope of obtaining his support at some point in return. Nothing is more contrary to the spirit of the council than a search which has not been purified by the sole desire to discern God's will.

If there is one time when it is important to seek peace and pursue it, to avoid disputes and the temptation to prove yourself right, it is during the council. Avoid a tone that precludes reply, the categorical "we must." Do not build up clever arguments to make yourself heard; express in a few words what you feel conforms most closely to God's plan, without imagining that you can impose it.

To avoid encouraging any spirit of rivalry, the servant of communion is responsible before his Lord for making decisions without being bound by a majority. Set free from human pressures, he listens with the same attention to the most timid brother as to a brother full of self-assurance. If he senses a lack of real agreement on an important question, he should reserve judgment and, in order to advance, make a provisional decision, ready to review it later; standing still is disobedience for brothers advancing toward Christ. He knows best what each one is capable of; if a brother is to be given a responsibility, he is the first to propose it.

The council is composed of the brothers who have made profession; brothers who are absent are consulted by the servant of communion or by a brother he has chosen.

Harmony

LIFE IN COMMUNITY is not possible without a minimum of harmony.

Why would you inconvenience your brothers by being late, or neglectful?

If some major reason demands your absence and you are unable to be present at an act of the community, do not excuse yourself through an intermediary.

Never be a hindrance by a lack of eagerness to return to the brothers with whom you have committed yourself totally, mind and body.

Throughout Your Day
Let Work And Rest
Be Quickened By The Word Of God

IN YOUR LIFE of prayer and meditation, look for the words God addresses to you and put them into practice at once. So read little, but take your time over it.

If your praying is to be genuine, you need to be at grips with the demands of work. A careless or half-hearted attitude would make you incapable of true intercession. Strive for regularity in your work. Your prayer becomes total when it is one with your work.

Hour by hour pray, work or rest, but all in God.

In the work you do, never make comparisons between yourself and the other brothers. Your place is necessary for the witness of the whole community—in all simplicity, know how to keep it.

Keep Inner Silence In All Things And You Will Dwell In Christ

INNER SILENCE REQUIRES us first to forget our own selves and so quieten conflicting voices and master obsessive anxiety, constantly beginning again, never discouraged because always forgiven. It makes possible our conversation with Jesus Christ.

But who does not dread this silence, preferring to relax when it is time for work, then fleeing prayer and wearing himself out at useless jobs, neglecting his neighbor and himself?

Your dialogue with Christ demands this silence. Unless you keep offering him everything, and talk to him with the simplicity of a child, how will you find inner unity when by nature you are anxious or complacent?

You fear that this inner silence may leave some question within you unsettled? Then make a note of what is troubling you or causing resentment; the solution can be found later.

There are times when the silence of God in his creatures comes to a climax. Alone in retreat, we are renewed by the intimate encounter with Christ.

Peace and quiet are important for love of the brothers who are praying, reading, writing or, in the evening, resting.

Discretion in speech or gesture has never prevented human contact; only mute silence could cause relationships to break down. That is not required of us, because by itself it is not conducive to the true spirit of inner silence.

Be Filled With The Spirit
Of The Beatitudes:
Joy, Simplicity, Mercy

Joy

In the communion of saints, day after day we sing the Lord's renewed compassion, and his mercy kindles our fervor.

True joy begins within.

Acting the fool has never restored joy. Remember that there is no clear dividing line between simple joking and the irony which turns a smile into a grimace. Mockery is cowardly because it serves to cloak so-called truths which nobody would dare to express in direct conversation.

Perfect joy lies in the utter simplicity of peaceful love. In order to shine out, such joy requires no less than your whole being.

Do not be afraid of sharing in others' trials, do not be afraid of suffering, for it is often in the depth of the abyss that we discover the perfection of joy in communion with Jesus Christ.

Perfect joy is self-giving. Whoever knows it seeks neither gratitude nor kindness. It is sheer wonder renewed by the sight of the generosity of the Giver of all gifts, material and spiritual. It is thankfulness. It is thanksgiving.

Simplicity

Availability means constantly simplifying your mode of living, not by constraint but by faith.

Flee the devious paths through which the tempter seeks you. Throw aside all useless burdens, the better to bring to Christ your Lord those of your fellow human beings.

In the transparency of brotherly love, admit your mistakes simply, never using them as a pretext for pointing out those of others. Wherever they are, brothers practice brief and frequent sharing together.

Simplicity is also loyalty toward oneself as a way of acquiring limpidity. It is a way of openness toward our neighbor.

Simplicity lies in the free joy of a brother who has given up any obsession with his own progress or backsliding to keep his eye fixed on the light of Christ.

Mercy

As peace with Christ involves peace with your neighbor, seek reconciliation, make amends where you can.

Forgive your brother seventy times seven times.

You may fear that a brother's pride will be flattered if you forget his offense: in that case exhort him, but only when the two of you are alone, and with the gentleness of Christ. If you refrain from doing so in order to safeguard your need of influence or popularity with certain brothers, you become an occasion of stumbling in the community.

Always be ready to forgive. Do not forget that love also finds expression in marks of mutual consideration. No weak sentimentality, and no harsh words. Consider when you speak impatiently how Christ is hurt.

Refuse to indulge in personal dislikes. They can easily flourish when the large number of brothers means that you cannot be open and free with everyone. Your natural inclinations may lead you to be prejudiced from the start, to judge your neighbor by his bad side. Let yourself be filled instead with an abundance of friendship for all.

Avoid petty disagreements between brothers. Nothing is more divisive than endless discussions about everything under the sun. See that you stop them when necessary. Refuse to listen to insinuations about a brother. Be a ferment of unity.

If you have doubts about a brother's attitude, and either you cannot talk to him about it or he refuses to listen to you, confide them to the servant of communion and see together what can be done to help that brother. Should he then refuse to listen to you both, tell the community.

Because of the weakness of your flesh, Christ offers you visible and repeated signs of forgiveness. Absolution restores you to the joy of a reconciliation. Still, you have to ask for it. The sin of one member marks the whole body, but God's forgiveness reintegrates into the community. Confession is made to one particular brother, chosen with the servant of communion.

Anyone who lives in mercy is neither oversensitive nor constantly disappointed. He gives himself simply, forgetting himself; joyfully, with all his heart; freely, not looking for anything in return.

Celibacy

CELIBACY BRINGS GREATER freedom to attend to the things of God, but it can only be accepted with the aim of giving ourselves more completely to our neighbor with the love of Christ himself.

Our celibacy means neither indifference nor a break with human affections; it calls for their transfiguration. Christ alone can convert our passions into total love of our neighbor. When selfishness is not transcended by growing generosity, when you no longer resort to confession to overcome the need for self-assertion contained in every passion, when the heart is not constantly brimming over with great love, you can no longer let Christ love in you, and your celibacy becomes a burden.

This working of Christ in you demands infinite patience.

Purity of heart is contrary to all natural tendencies.

Impurity, even in the imagination, leaves psychological traces which are not always removed instantly by confession and absolution. The main thing is to keep living new beginnings as a Christian never disheartened because always forgiven.

Purity of heart is closely linked with transparency. Do not display your difficulties, but do not withdraw either as though you were superhuman and exempt from struggles.

Refuse to connive in vulgarity. Certain jokes can revive the difficulties of brothers who are striving to remain pure in heart.

There is a slackness of attitude which could veil the true meaning of the difficult yet joyful commitment of chastity. Remember that your behavior and your bearing are signs; neglect of them can hinder us on our way forward together.

Purity of heart can only be lived in spontaneous, joyful self-forgetting, as we give our lives for those we love. Giving ourselves in this way means accepting that our susceptibilities will often be wounded.

There is no friendship without purifying suffering.

There is no love for our neighbor without the Cross. Only by the Cross can we know the unfathomable depths of love.

Community Of Goods

THE POOLING OF goods is total.

The audacity involved in putting to good use all that is available at any time, not laying up capital and not fearing possible poverty, is a source of incalculable strength.

But if, like Israel, you save the bread from heaven for tomorrow, you are in danger of pointlessly overstraining the brothers whose vocation is to live in the present.

Poverty has no virtue in itself.

The poor of the Gospel learn to live without having the next day's needs ensured, joyfully confident that everything will be provided.

The spirit of poverty does not mean looking poverty-stricken, but disposing everything in creation's simple beauty.

The spirit of poverty means living in the joyfulness of each present day. If for God there is the generosity of distributing all the good things of the earth, for human beings there is the grace of giving what they have received.

The Servant Of Communion

WITHOUT UNITY, there is no hope for bold and total service of Jesus Christ. Individualism breaks up the community and brings it to a halt.

The servant of communion inspires unity within the community.

He points the way in matters of practical detail, but for every important question he listens to the council before making a decision.

The brothers should remain spontaneous with him; but remembering that the Lord has entrusted him with a charge, they should be attentive to all that concerns his ministry.

By their attitude of trust, the brothers renew the servant of communion in the seriousness of his vocation for the joy of all; by their spirit of petty demands, they paralyze his ministry.

Each brother should frankly tell the servant of communion, in private, the fears he may have. Revolt expressed before others is bound to contaminate, and it is here that the tempter finds his best weapons to divide what must remain one. Beware of childish reactions which accuse others when it would be more appropriate first to accuse ourselves.

The spirit of perfection, if that means imposing one's own point of view as the best, is a scourge in the community. True perfection, precisely, is bearing the imperfections of our neighbor, out of love.

The servant of communion is subject to the same failings as his broth-

ers. If they love him for his human qualities, they risk no longer accepting him in his ministry when they discover his faults.

The servant of communion appoints a brother to ensure continuity
after him.

Making decisions is a formidable task for the servant of communion.

He should keep alert and pray so as to build up the whole body in
Christ.

He should look for the special gifts of each brother, so that the
brother can discern them for himself.

He should not consider his charge to be superior, nor must he as-
sume it in a spirit of resignation. He should bear in mind only that it has
been entrusted to him by Christ, to whom he will have to give account.

He should root out all authoritarianism in himself, but never be
weak, in order to maintain his brothers in God's plan. He should pre-
vent the authoritarian from dominating and give confidence to the
weak.

He should arm himself with mercy and ask Christ to grant it as the
grace most essential for him.

Brothers On Mission

LIKE THE DISCIPLES sent out two by two, brothers on mission are
witnesses to Christ, called to be a sign of his presence among all and
bearers of joy.

Everywhere and at all times, they represent the community; the witness of the whole body depends on their attitude. They keep the servant
of communion regularly informed about their life. They should not
venture into any new project without his agreement, as he is responsible for consulting others. If brothers on mission fail to keep this close
contact, they very soon break the unity of the body.

If they are two or more, the servant of communion designates one of them to be in charge.

Their spiritual life is that of the community.

Welcoming

TO PREPARE HIMSELF to follow Christ, each new brother requires time to mature.

He should beware of the illusion that he has now arrived. Even if he assimilates rapidly, he needs time to understand the vocation in its utmost consequences.

As long as we are not known by new brothers, we are tempted to monopolize them for ourselves. We should remember that there are brothers appointed to listen to them and to prepare them for profession.

Guests

IN EACH GUEST it is Christ himself whom we have to receive; so let us learn to be welcoming and be ready to offer our free time. Our hospitality should be generous and discerning.

During meals the brothers should be attentive to the presence of a guest and be careful not to disconcert him.

Certain brothers are responsible for the welcome while other brothers continue with their work. This helps to avoid dilettantism.

Conclusion

PERHAPS IT IS risky to have indicated in these pages only the essentials for a common life. Better run this risk, and not settle into complacency and routine.

If this rule were ever to be regarded as an end in itself, dispensing us from always searching to discover more of God's plan, more of the love of Christ, more of the light of the Holy Spirit, we would be laying a useless burden on our shoulders: better, then, never to have written it.

If Christ is to grow in me, I must know my own weakness and that of my brothers. For them I will become all things to all, and give even my life, for Christ's sake and the Gospel's.

Exhortation Read At Profession

BROTHER, what do you ask?

The mercy of God and the community of my brothers.

May God complete in you what he has begun.

Brother, you trust in God's mercy: remember that the Lord Christ comes to help the weakness of your faith; committing himself with you, he fulfills for you his promise:

"Truly, there is no one who has given up home, brothers, sisters, mother, father, wife or children for my sake and the Gospel's, who will not receive a hundred times as much at present—homes and brothers and sisters and mothers and children—and persecutions too, and in the age to come eternal life."

This is a way contrary to all human reason; like Abraham you can only advance along it by faith, not by sight, always sure that whoever loses his life for Christ's sake will find it.

From now on walk in the steps of Christ. Do not be anxious about tomorrow. First seek God's Kingdom and its justice. Surrender yourself, give yourself, and good measure, pressed down, shaken together, brimming over, will be poured out for you; the measure you give is the measure you will receive.

Whether you wake or sleep, night and day the seed springs up and grows, you do not know how.

Avoid parading your goodness before people to gain their admiration. Never let your inner life make you look sad, like a hypocrite who puts on a grief-stricken air to attract attention. Anoint your head and wash your face, so that only your Father who is in secret knows what your heart intends.

Stay simple and full of joy, the joy of the merciful, the joy of brotherly love.

Be vigilant. If you have to rebuke a brother, keep it between the two of you.

Be concerned to establish communion with your neighbor.

Be open about yourself, remembering that you have a brother whose charge it is to listen to you. Bring him your understanding so that he can fulfill his ministry with joy.

The Lord Christ, in his compassion and his love for you, has chosen you to be in the Church a sign of brotherly love. It is his will that with your brothers you live the parable of community.

So, refusing to look back, and joyful with infinite gratitude, never fear to outstrip the dawn,

praising
blessing
and singing
Christ your Lord.

The Commitments Made At Profession

RECEIVE ME, Lord, and I will live; may my expectation be a source of joy.

Brother, remember that it is Christ who calls you and that it is to him that you are now going to respond.

Will you, for love of Christ, consecrate yourself to him with all your being?

I will.

Will you henceforth fulfill your service of God within our community, in communion with your brothers?

I will.

Will you, renouncing all ownership, live with your brothers not only in community of material goods but also in community of spiritual goods, striving for openness of heart?

I will.

Will you, in order to be more available to serve with your brothers, and in order to give yourself in undivided love to Christ, remain in celibacy?

I will.

Will you, so that we may be of one heart and one mind and so that the unity of our common service may be fully achieved, adopt the orientations of the community expressed by the servant of communion, bearing in mind that he is only a poor servant in the community?

I will.

Will you, always discerning Christ in your brothers, watch over them in good days and bad, in suffering and in joy?

I will.

In consequence, because of Christ and the Gospel, you are henceforth a brother of our community.

TWO

LET CHRIST TRANSFIGURE IN US THE SHADOWS THEMSELVES

Celebrate The Moment With God

Without looking back, you want to follow Christ: here and now, in the present moment, turn to God and trust in the Gospel. In so doing, you draw from the sources of jubilation.

You think you do not know how to pray. Yet the Risen Christ is there; he loves you before you love him. By "his Spirit who dwells in our hearts," he intercedes in you far more than you can imagine.

Even without recognizing him, learn to wait for him with or without words, during long silences when nothing seems to happen. There obsessive discouragements vanish, creative impulses well up. Nothing can be built up in you without this adventure—finding him in the intimacy of a personal encounter. No one can do it for you.

When you have trouble understanding what he wants of you, tell him so. In the course of daily activities, at every moment, tell him all, even things you cannot bear.

Do not compare yourself with others, and with what they can do.

Why wear yourself out regretting what is impossible for you? Could you have forgotten God? Turn to him. No matter what happens, dare to begin over and over again.

If you were to accuse yourself of all that is in you, your days and nights would not suffice. You have something better to do: in the present moment, celebrate God's forgiveness, despite the resistances to believing yourself forgiven, whether by God or by others.

When inner trials or incomprehensions from without make themselves felt, remember that in the very same wound where the poison of anxiety festers, there too the energies for loving are born.

If you seem to be walking in a thick fog, waiting for him, Christ, means giving him the time to put everything in its place . . . A fountain of gladness will spring up in the desert of your heart. Not a euphoric bliss, not just any kind of joy, but that jubilation which comes straight from the wellsprings of Eternity.

The Silence Of Contemplation

PRAYER, descending into the depths of God, is not there to make life easy for us. Prayer: not for any kind of result, but in order to create with Christ a communion in which we are free.

When we strive to give expression to this communion in words, we have conscious prayers. But our understanding can only express the outer surface of ourselves. Very soon it comes up short . . . and silence remains, to such an extent as to seem a sign of the absence of God.

Instead of coming to a standstill with the barrenness of silence, know that it opens toward unheard-of possibilities of creation: in the underlying world of the human person, in what lies beyond our consciousness, Christ prays, more than we can imagine. Compared with the vastness of this secret prayer of Christ in us, our explicit praying dwindles to almost nothing.

Certainly, the essence of prayer takes place above all in a great silence . . .

All prayer remains arduous for any who are left to themselves. God has made us social beings, and has given us a "political" calling. Could this be why contemplation becomes less of an effort when it is lived in fellowship with others?

The silence of contemplation! Within each of us lie unknown gulfs of doubt, violence, secret distress . . . and also chasms of guilt, of things unacknowledged, so that gaping below our feet we sense an immense void. Our impulses seethe; we do not know their origin; perhaps they come from some ancestral or genetic memory. So let Christ pray in us, trusting as a child, and one day these gulfs will be inhabited.

One day, later on, we shall discover that there has been a revolution in ourselves.

With time, contemplation begets a happiness. And that happiness is the drive behind our struggle for and with all people. It is courage, energy to take risks. It is overflowing gladness.

The contemplative life is not an existence hovering between heaven and earth, in ecstasy or illumination. It begins when in humility we come closer to God and to our neighbor. It is always stamped with the seal of a practical mind.

It lays down one condition: keep inner silence at all times. There are ways of attaining this, at work or when alone: frequently invoking the name of Jesus, saying or singing a Psalm you know by heart, or making the simple gesture of the sign of the cross.

It is also a certain way of looking at one's neighbor, a vision transfigured by reconciliation. Anyone who is continually faced with a variety of different individuals finds refreshment in these children of God; fatigue itself is swept away when they are accepted with an attentiveness constantly renewed at the wellsprings of contemplation.

Contemplative waiting upon God leads us to the acceptances necessary each day: acceptance of our state of life, our growing older, acceptance of opportunities lost. Regret itself is transformed into a dynamic act, repentance, which stimulates our advance.

In *Thomas Gordeyev,* Gorky tells how on the Volga ice destroyed Ignatius' boat. A miser who watched every ruble, he accepted the loss instantly. He knew regret would be useless, and already he felt reassured and encouraged by the thought of the new boat he was going to build.

In regret the inner self disintegrates. Far from being stimulated, our spirit becomes sterile when it keeps on reconstructing a situation that is over and done with, giving itself over to fruitless brooding.

Some people have had a childhood that encourages unconscious remorse. We would all like to begin over again and do better. But is there anything we do really well? We live and work in the realm of the approximate. Regret sterilizes the impulse to create. Regret debilitates.

If we are granted a time of certainty, security and sure ground, it is when we are gathered together in contemplative waiting on God. Then, everything is possible once more. Even the salt recovers its savor; what was insipid has value again.

In contemplative waiting all our innate pessimism dissolves, even if this pessimism is rooted in what we actually see in society and in ourselves.

There are so many reasons for pessimism in the world today. There are the masses of people, increasing day by day, without any sense of God, and the Christian societies which are turned in upon themselves. There is the prospect of seeing, twenty years from now, four billion human beings living in deprivation, while one billion live in plenty. There is the huge wave slowly breaking over us: a technological civilization encapsulating us and submerging us in its totality.

There are also inner grounds for discouragement: the combat we live day after day, and the old self that refuses to submit—the pride of life, the stubborn will which persists in taking no account of its neighbor, the weight of fatigue. So many reasons in life for pessimism.

In contemplative waiting upon God everything becomes desirable again. Pessimism is watered down and yields to the optimism of faith. Then and only then is it possible to consider what is coming toward us and to welcome the events of the present time, to run toward our neighbor, to make a new start, to go forward. It is only in contemplative waiting upon God that we can find new momentum.

Wait!

Wait for the dawning of a life, when God will gather us into his arms forever.

Wait for God to act, in ourselves and in others.

Wait for a communion within the People of God which will spark a communion among all people.

Wait for the springtime of the Church.

Wait, in spite of everything, for the spirit of mercy; for love which is not a consuming fire is not charity, and without charity we would be professing ecumenism without hope.

God is preparing us for a new Pentecost which will set every one of us ablaze with the fire of his love. Our part is to run and meet the event which will upset all our human calculations and bring life to our dry bones.

Run toward, not away!

Run to meet the world's tomorrow, a technological civilization fully charged with potential for human development.

Run to meet all who cannot believe, and to struggle alongside the most exploited.

Run to support a rebirth of the People of God, asking and imploring them, in season and out of season, to come together, and so to raise up in the world an unmistakable sign of our brotherly love.

The Essential Hidden From Our Eyes

A Life from Elsewhere
Prayer is both struggle and surrender. Prayer is also waiting, waiting for a way through, waiting for the walls of our inner resistance to break

down. In the same way, Christ in his earthly life knew times of intense patience.

Prayer is an astonishing thing. It propels us elsewhere, out of ourselves. Christ is recognized in our neighbor, to be sure, and he is always alive within us; but he is elsewhere too, present in his own right.

Prayer is always poor; we who live it are poor servants to the very end. Prayer will always exceed our powers. Words are unfit to describe it. In prayer there lies something beyond what we are, beyond our own words.

For all of us, meaning in language is so important. It is easy to understand that, on approaching this fluid realm where everything seems to happen in the incommunicable, the first reaction of many is repulsion or fear.

It was so from the very beginnings of Christian history: "We do not know how to pray, but the Holy Spirit comes to the help of our inadequacy and prays in us."

Prayer never changes in its essence through the centuries, but it adopts different forms as history unfolds, or at different periods of our lives.

Some pray with no words. All is wrapped in a great silence.

Others use very many words to express themselves. In the sixteenth century Teresa of Ávila, a woman of great courage and realism, wrote of prayer: "When I speak to the Lord, I often do not know what I am saying. It is love that speaks. And the soul is so beside itself that I can see no difference between it and God. Love forgets itself and says foolish things."

Others find in the liturgy, or in common prayer, the joy of heaven on earth, a fulfillment . . .

There are some who repeat over and over again a few words they have learned to stammer. Through this prayer of repetition, a prayer suitable for the poor—and we are all of us poor—the whole being is brought into unity. Some repeat the humble greeting of Elizabeth to Mary, "Hail Mary . . ." Those may be the only words they have left when they are caught off their guard by human distress. Or else they murmur, audibly or not, to the rhythm of their breathing, the prayer of the Name of Jesus. To all appearances, the endless repetition of the same words lacks spontaneity. Yet, after long waiting, life comes surging up within, a fullness, the Holy Spirit's unsettling presence.

What of those others who practically never experience any detectable resonance of a presence in them? Their whole life long they are in waiting, and that is the fire behind their seeking. Contemplation is a struggle, it does not bring immediate fullness flooding over them, it does not arouse any spontaneous outburst of feeling for Christ.

Many are the ways of prayer. Some follow one, others pursue them all. There are moments of bright certainty—Christ is there, speaking within us. But there are other moments when he is Silence, a distant stranger . . . No one is privileged in prayer.

In all its infinite variety, prayer brings us across to a life not our own, a life from elsewhere.

Another's Looking

What distinguishes a person who builds his entire life on the challenge of prayer from somebody who is indifferent to it? To the outward eye, nothing. The person who prays is the same as everyone else, getting up each morning, walking around, eating . . . But within, there is all the difference in the world. For that person, the challenge of prayer is a creation more essential than the events of his or her own history.

If prayer were aimed at some practical goal, what a mockery it would be! Nothing but a projection of self, even a bargaining-match with God!

Whether serene contemplation or inner struggle, prayer is just learning to place everything in other hands, with the simplicity of a child.

Through the steadfastness of prayer, each one finds energy for other struggles—for supporting a family or for transforming social conditions . . . Far from withdrawing or escaping from events and from people, a person of prayer learns to consider them with eyes informed by Another's looking.

When we are desperately self-seeking, when we cannot tear our eyes away from ourselves, the pride of life sweeps us along with its inevitable accompaniment of ambition, careerism and the longing to be a success. But if, on the contrary, we let Another use our eyes, then nothing but the unique reality will count.

Everything depends on how we look at ourselves, other people and events. So much so, that almost everything that happens to us arises out of ourselves. Either the pride of life is the driving force of our existence, and all that counts is domination of people and things, by money but also without money. Or Christ's looking takes the place of our own: then the way lies open for the gift of our lives.

The Gateways of Praise

Someone dear to me gave me an account one day of a whole inner battle:

"I have known what it is to be tempted by self-analysis—all its question marks, its incessant who-are-you's and its endless whys. This sort of questioning can sometimes lead to vanity, but more often than not the result is sadness, shame and self-contempt. So I kept turning over the earth of my being, working at it in an attempt to make it more and more beautiful, until in the end I had made the beauty of my earth a goal in itself, forgetting that the aim is to sow a seed of the Gospel in it.

"I knew the words in Isaiah, 'You shall call your gateways praise.' But I called mine introspection, anguish and scruple. On my gateways was written, 'I am no more worthy to be called your son.' Those are narrow gates, not opening outward at all, but inward to the lowest levels of the self.

"From now on I shall call my gateways praise. Those gateways open wide toward the outside world, toward him who is beyond all things and beyond myself."

When introspection and analysis turn us in on ourselves, what destruction that brings! Who then will open for us the gateways of praise?

Shortly before he died in 1943, a political prisoner in southern Spain, Miguel Hernandez, unveiled a certain secret:

> Open, Love, in me the gates
> of the perfect wound;
> Open, to release
> the useless anguish;
> Open, see, coming,
> the breath of your word.

The gateways of praise give passage to deathly anguish and to songs unending. God will set his mark on the very wounds themselves, making them no longer torment, but energy for communion.

To want a life with no contradictions, shocks, opposition, with no criticism, is to fall into disincarnate dreaming. Confronted with the shaking of foundations, in ourselves, in the Church or in human society, we are offered two ways.

Either hurt and anguish pass into bitterness, when, groaning under the crushing load, we become rooted to the spot and all is lost.

Or else pain and sadness find an outlet in the praise of His love, lifting us out of passivity and enabling us to deal with anything that comes our way.

From Doubt Toward Believing

NO ONE IS built naturally for living the radicalism of the Gospel. In every person the yes and the no are superimposed.

Yet it is through giving ourselves totally that we grow. If we risk our whole life, that becomes the preparation for events beyond our wildest hopes. Situations of standstill, discouragement or fierce struggle, far from demolishing, build us up. The ways through darkness are traveled stage by stage—the solitude of the long, dim nights, with human thirsts unquenched . . . bitterness, that gangrene of the heart . . . storms . . . all the fears that crouch at life's turning points . . .

What if the ground is overgrown with thorns, scrubwood and briars? With thorns, Christ lights a fire. Are there still roots of bitterness, is love still impossible? That goes to feed the fire. Weakness becomes a crucible where the yes is made and re-made and made new day after day. What most threatens us is transformed into a means of lightening our heaviness.

The moment comes when we receive what we no longer even expected. What we had never dared to hope for arises. A gleam of Christ in us. Others see it shining, although we are unaware of it. Nothing is to be gained by knowing what light we reflect; many people already reflect God's brightness without knowing it, perhaps even without daring to believe it.

For those who risk their whole lives, no road ever comes to a dead end.

We think we have abandoned Christ, but he does not abandon us.

We think that we have forgotten him, but he was there.

And we set out once more, we begin all over again: he is present.

That is the unexpected; that is what we had not dared hope for.

Confronted with the radicalism of the Gospel and the risks it implies, many people take fright. Doubt remains. Some do not know if they are still believers or not.

It is never Christ who is absent or far away from us; we are the ones who are distracted, far off or indifferent. Christ exists in his own right, he is not confined to the subjective feelings we may or may not have of him.

If we are more aware of doubt now than in the past, this is the result of our greater readiness to accept that pockets of incredulity remain in us.

In the past, "I believe," "Credo," sprang more easily to the lips; today, many prefer to tell God first "I love you" and then, much later on, "I believe."

More than a century ago, at a moment when Christians were for the first time asking such questions about doubt and faith, Dostoyevsky wrote from his Siberian prison: "I am a child of disbelief and doubt, to this very hour and even, I am sure, to my last breath. How great are the sufferings I have had to endure from this thirst to believe, which only grows stronger in my soul with the growth in me of arguments to the contrary." Yet Dostoyevsky goes on to insist that, in his eyes, "There is nothing more beautiful, more profound, more congenial, more reasonable, more virile, more perfect than Christ and not only is there nothing, but with a jealous love I say that there can be nothing. Still more, if someone were to demonstrate to me that Christ is outside of truth, and that truth really lies outside of Christ, I would rather stay with Christ than with truth."

When Dostoyevsky suggests that the nonbeliever coexists in him with the believer, the no with the yes, his passionate love for Christ still remains undiminished. Child of doubt and disbelief, he nonetheless hears Christ's "Do you love me?" and returns, day after day, to the journey from doubt toward believing.

In Everyone, A Unique Gift

LIKE EACH AND every one of us, Jesus needed to hear a human voice saying, "You know that I love you." Three times over he repeated to Peter: "Do you love me?" Assured of Peter's love, Jesus entrusted him with the Church: "Feed my sheep."

To love Christ is to receive from him, immediately, a greater or lesser share in a pastoral gift. God entrusts to everybody one or more other persons.

This pastoral gift, however small, is a source from which to draw the inspirations to communicate Christ. It allows us to accomplish our pilgrimage in the whole human family.

Children themselves, without being aware of it, transmit an image of the living God.

Exercising this pastoral gift means above all listening. Listening to what in others hurts them about themselves. Trying to understand what is beneath others' hearts until even in earth harrowed by tribulations they can perceive God's hope, or at least human hope.

And it often happens that the one who listens to another is in fact led to the essential, and the other never even suspects it.

Growing old. Exercising intuition during a whole lifetime of listening. And in the end understanding, almost without words, those who confide in one.

Listening can bring a mystical vision of the human being, that creature inhabited by both frailty and radiance, fullness and void.

In each one, a share in a pastoral heart. In each person, unique gifts. Why doubt one's own gifts so much? Why, in comparing oneself with others, desire their gifts and go so far as to bury one's own?

Today a technological age intensifies an acute sense of success and failure. A disposition to get on in the world and to compare oneself with others is inculcated from childhood. Those who do not succeed according to society's standards feel condemned and disappointed that they do not have somebody else's gifts.

Comparisons sterilize. Wishing for another's abilities induces us to become incapable of discovering the gifts in ourselves. Discredit yourself and up come sadness and discouragement.

How is it possible to lose self-esteem, when the Spirit of life is pouring gifts into every one of us? The loss of self-esteem suffocates a human being, shackles vital energies, and goes so far as to make it impossible to create.

To react against this by overestimating oneself—by seeking social prestige, for instance—is not a way out. Overestimating oneself under social pressure or because of the judgments of those around us, forcing one's gifts artificially, would be like forcing a plant in a hothouse.

There is a way in the Gospel where we meet the gaze of Christ. It has a name: the way of consenting. Consenting to one's own limitations, of intelligence, faith and ability. Consenting also to one's own talents. That is how strong creations come to birth.

You Want To Be Fully Alive

YOU WANT TO be fully alive, and not half dead. Did you know that "The glory of God is a human being fully alive. The life of a human being is the vision of God"?

Together with many others throughout the earth, will you place your confidence in the living God? Will you find the meaning of your life and a serene joy in him?

When this confidence disappears among believers, deserts of scepticism and doubt invade large regions of the world.

In these dry lands, some Christians are even mistrustful of one another, divided by old or entirely new conflicts.

If, at the heart of such situations, you live as someone who is already reconciled, you will discover that it is as if you were in the catacombs and you will pray: "My soul thirsts for the living God, when will I see him face to face?"

During the time of the catacombs, Christians drew their courage from the very heart of the faith. Subjected to the strongest pressures, they understood that the meaning of existence in the Gospel is to "give one's life."

Yes, the Gospel puts each of us before a choice: either to give one's life, not in several parts, but one's entire existence, or to serve oneself and follow one's own shadow—for example, in the pursuit of human prestige.

It is impossible to walk on these two ways at the same time. To choose Christ means following only one. Will you choose Christ?

Begin. Place your confidence in him. Do not wait for your heart to be changed; Christ will change it day after day.

When tensions, discouragements and doubts seem to disrupt everything, can you glimpse an inner light?

In the desert of the heart, when all doors seem closed, the moment comes when, without knowing how, you are brought back to what matters most: in following Christ, you are there "to give your life, to serve, not to be served." No one can find a stronger meaning to existence, nor a greater love.

Then, unimagined resources are liberated from within you, flowing without drying up. And the desert flower blooms.

You do not want to be half dead, but fully alive. Have you understood that the desire for the Spirit, the desire for the living God, leads you to life and to peace?

Perhaps you will say: How can one desire God without yet knowing him?

Open the Scriptures. The living God is perceived in Christ Jesus, the Risen Lord.

Approach the Eucharist with the simplicity of a child's heart. Little by little you will understand.

In order to begin again each day, place your confidence in the Holy Spirit. The Spirit dwells in your heart.

Do not rely only on your own faith. Lean on those who have gone before you and on those who accompany you today.

Seek God through forgiveness. At times you feel too full of guilt to believe in God's forgiveness. You say to yourself: surely God forgives others, but not me. Do not forget that the sure mark of God is that, like all love, his love is forgiveness. If you stopped short in fear of being punished, how would you be able to love God?

The inner life resumes its course when, forgiven by God, you have forgiven your brother or sister. For those who offer others the forgiveness which God has given them, there is a springtime of the heart.

No longer looking back, at every moment casting your own and your neighbor's past into the water of Baptism and turning toward what lies before you, live in the present moment. Yes, let today be enough for you; and an inner creation which will never end is brought to fulfillment within you, leading to eternal life.

In order to seek God, watch and pray. If you think that you do not know how to pray, are you going to give up because of that? Remain before God without words. And, if you can, speak to Christ Jesus simply and humbly. A single word is enough, especially if it comes from your depths.

In prayer, you will be surprised at times, saying: "My thoughts wander and my heart goes astray." The Gospel answers you: "God is greater than your heart." At every moment, abandon yourself in body and spirit. Entrust to God all that burdens you. Dare to say to him: "Give me the gift of giving myself." Sing together with others to the point of discovering the desire for God.

No one can separate prayer and action. It should never be struggle *or* contemplation, but one *with* the other, one flowing from the other. The Risen Lord accompanies you everywhere, not only at church, but also in the street, and at work.

Contemplation—not in order to close your eyes before all that threatens or assails the weak of the world, nor to the sin of war. Contemplation is a serene force which works and prepares the ground within you.

Let Christ Transfigure In Us
The Shadows Themselves

OUTSIDE OF THE light of Christ we are shrouded in darkness. This is true for us all and will always be so. We simply feel it more deeply at certain stages of our life or at certain periods in human history.

If we enter a church in the East or the West during the Easter vigil, we may find ourselves in the company of believers who have come in the silence of night or early morning, like the women who, on the eve of Christ's resurrection, came to the tomb while it was still dark. When the cantor sings "Light of Christ" and lights a candle in the middle of the congregation, those present answer "Thanks be to God." This happens three times. It is thanksgiving for the resurrection.

The light of the Transfiguration of Christ tells us that already today the work of the resurrection has begun in us.

The apostle Peter was present at the Transfiguration and in one of his letters he tells us the meaning of the event. In so doing he reveals to us a basic dimension of the Christian life.

We are in the night. In the depth of this darkness a small flame is burning. All we have to do is to keep our eyes focused on that light, "until the day breaks and the morning star rises in our hearts."

Why should we go far away looking for what is so close at hand? At times, wanting to bypass faith and patience, we demand wonders and miracles, immediately visible signs. But we have to contemplate that light with perseverance before the morning star can rise. As we remain in God's presence, we have to see everything from now on in the light of Christ; to view our neighbor in that way, our own self, and all of life.

—To view our neighbor in that light. To know that in every human being, even in one who does not profess faith in Christ, a reflection of the very image of the Creator shines forth. Our neighbor is not necessarily the man or woman who spontaneously appeals to us, but the one wounded by life, lying beside our road. Our neighbor is not only the person for whom we have an immediate feeling of friendship, but also the one who, because we are indifferent to him or her, deserves more than anyone else to be contemplated with the eyes of Christ himself.

—Viewing Christians in that light. This means first of all seeing them as bearers of Christ, and then ceasing to complain about all that may be negative in them, focusing our attention instead on the gifts, the positive work of Christ, the little light that has been placed in them. Nothing is more refreshing than to discover the hope alive in a witness to God who has been mistreated by life.

—Viewing ourselves as well in the light of Christ. Instead of letting ourselves be brought to a standstill because in us there is—and there always will be—evil, impossibilities, darkness, shadows, some have learned how to lay down this burden by making use of confession. When they have received forgiveness, at once they make it the wellspring of their life, for a Christian's life is not rooted in beating one's breast or in feelings of guilt, but in Christ shining in us like a tiny light in the midst of the shadows.

—Viewing and contemplating all of life, all of creation, in this light from God, since at its origin all of creation was willed in the fullness of God.

A plant not turned toward the light withers. In the same way, a Christian who refuses to look at God's light, and who instead wants only to see the shadows, is doomed to a slow death. Such a person cannot grow and be built up in Christ.

The apostles, led away to the mountaintop, were given a visible glimpse of what was meant for them on the day when they would be one with Christ in God.

Little by little Christ transforms and transfigures in us all the rebellious, contradictory forces, all those murky and semiconscious states that remain deep within us and over which our will sometimes has no control at all.

As a result, it is possible to affirm to some who are convinced their life has been a failure that in the patience of God nothing is lost. Outstanding Christians like St. John of the Cross and St. Teresa of Ávila began a new life fairly late; they led many women and men to Christ, and so spoke about the fire kindled with all the wood of their past.

For those who are marked by suffering and by the cross of Christ: the day will come when they will burn with that flame fueled with their entire past life. On that day they will know that nothing exists without a meaning, and also that in God nothing is lost.

The light of Christ transfigures in us the shadows themselves. And yet these shadows are there; often we can do nothing about them. But by a slow maturation of the life of Christ in us, what was dark, unclear, opaque and even distressing is quietly illuminated and taken up in God. Nothing is lost on this earth because God is strong enough to give us back everything—transmuted, invigorated, transfigured by him. For this to happen, however, we must want to turn toward the light.

Just as the light of Christ is at work in the depths of our inner darkness, it is active as well in the dark places of the world. In this way God takes up an unbelieving humanity: by living in the midst of people unable to believe, Christians are bearers of Christ. In utter discretion they communicate the very presence of God.

The apostles contemplated the transfigured Christ and, knowing that it was one of the most important moments of their life, they wanted to remain in that dazzling light. But they had to come down off the mountaintop, and henceforth see the light of Christ shining in the Church that was just coming into being, in themselves and in the world.

And this is true for every Christian: we have to come down to earth to let God shine forth in our lives without the noise of words, so that by the light of Christ in us, all may glimpse the source of our visible unity. By it, those who cannot believe will be led, without knowing how, toward God's own hope.

THREE

AT THE HEART OF THE CHURCH

Church, Become What You Are
In Your Depths

Church, become what you are in your depths: a land of the living, a land of reconciliation, a land of simplicity.

Church, "land of the living," open the doors of an inner life, that everyone be not half dead but fully alive.

Throw open the doors of joy. Enable us to glimpse something of heaven's joy on earth by means of an all-embracing, meditative prayer, which gathers together people of all ages, and where the singing never comes to an end.

Church, be a land of reconciliation.

There will never be a widespread awakening of Christians unless they live as people who are reconciled.

Once you are transfigured by a reconciliation which is not put off until later, you will be a leaven of trust and peace between peoples.

Church, be a land of simplicity.

The use of simple means promotes a life of communion, whereas exterior signs of power undermine trust and arouse fear.

Do not forget the hopes of so many persons who are deeply concerned that a way be found to share the world's wealth more equally. The inequality which exists is one of the sources of armed conflict. Be a land of sharing in order to be also a land of peace.

That Unique Communion
Called The Church

Weaving the Robe of Christ

Over the past fifteen years, new separations between Christians have been added to the old divisions of history. Many have lost interest in a visible communion of the People of God, to such an extent that the glorification of splits and oppositions has at times even become a new orthodoxy.

How aware are we that when divisions occur, there comes a time when it is too late to stop the process of splitting up? Freeing ourselves from suspicion in order to reconcile human beings who are torn apart involves a struggle to begin over and over again in transparency of heart, far from all dealing, scheming and self-interested calculations.

Searching for reconciliation, of course, never means taking the easy way out. If it put people to sleep, anesthetized their energies, led them to a suffocating resignation, it would be the very opposite of reconciliation.

The ecumenical vocation had the mission of bringing together separated Christians. But after some real advances, things came to a standstill. Ecumenical dialogues went on and on, setting Christians on parallel tracks, and nothing more.

Today, the current which glorified oppositions is losing force, and so the ecumenical vocation could find a way out of its impasse. But we are still in the desert . . . In the aridity of the desert, God speaks, but the language he speaks in is his language, not ours.

Some people, often sincerely concerned with finding a way out of the impasse, resolutely entered upon ways which cut them off from the rest of the People of God.

For the same reason, others sent up trial balloons. They were aware of the risks involved—those balloons might explode as they gained height. But their principal concern was to remain at the heart of God's People, in order to bring it new life from within.

The attempt to make communion among Christians visible involves remaining on the inside, just as a human being can only be changed from within, never by criticisms coming from without. Harshness and pressures have always been stepping-stones to blackmail, an attack on human freedom.

Re-creating bonds of communion means weaving threads—sometimes just a single thread, but that is already enough. Then what is being woven, whether we know it or not, is the robe of Christ, his Church.

A Communion Extended to All Dimensions

Why are we so concerned about that unique communion called the Church? It is because there can be no continuity of Christ in human history without Christians who are part of a people. Loving Christ in isolation closes us up in our own private world. Loving Christ, loving the communion in his Body, the Church, opens unlimited vistas before us.

And why are we so passionately concerned about the catholicity of the Church, that universality extended to all its dimensions: the dimension of depth which is the search for a face-to-face Encounter in contemplation; the dimension of breadth which is solidarity with the victimized; the dimension of height which is creativity in simple beauty, in common prayer?

This catholicity does not concern us on its own account. As soon as the Church becomes an end in itself, it is doomed to pettiness, to all kinds of definitive judgments that split it into fragments—into confessions, small or large.

The Church does not interest us on her own account, but only when she stimulates us to look for God at the wellsprings of adoration, when she motivates us to live Christ for others and when she becomes a place of communion for all humanity.

That unique communion called the Church holds no interest for us unless it is universal, ecumenical, catholic, able to take upon itself the distress and the hope of the whole human community. Not a place reserved for a few privileged people, for elites of the faith, but one which is open to all of us, the poor of this earth.

No matter how open it is, of course, the Church has contours, the contours of a body. But it holds no interest unless those who make it up are brothers and sisters of all, including nonbelievers.

Today the Church is faced with one of the great challenges of her history: is she sufficiently aware that she remains the only place capable of being a ferment of universal communion and of friendship in the human family as a whole?

For this ferment to reach all humanity, there is a prerequisite: a reconciliation between Christians that comes about without delay. How can unreconciled people profess allegiance to a God of love and awaken others to God by the lives they lead? Can Christians honestly continue to talk about ecumenism if they do not achieve reconciliation, concretely and without delay? If they only love those who love them and who resemble them, are not unbelievers capable of doing as much? The inconsistency represented by the divisions between Christians makes their words hardly credible, and turns the younger generations away from the Church.

A Church Devoid of Powerful Means

Some members of the younger generation love the Church but with a blind passion. And so they are deeply disturbed when they see individual Christians, or institutions, quick to profit from the ease offered by abundant material resources, be they buildings, capital held in reserve, or financial investments.

Long before Christ's coming, the prophet Jeremiah pronounced these challenging words: "My people have abandoned the source of living water; they have exchanged the radiance of God for cisterns that cannot hold water." And today there are young people who ask themselves similar questions. Is the absolute of God, his radiance, being exchanged for cisterns that do not contain living water? Whether in the short or in the long run, powerful means and authoritarian methods mean the death of communion.

The young are no more simplistic than their elders. It is not a matter of rejecting the display of artistic splendor in churches built down through the ages. When there is no artistic creation, puritanical and sectarian tendencies develop; they dehumanize and put pressure on people by creating guilty consciences. It is, rather, a matter of disposing everything in creation's simple beauty, and art too is a gift from God. Simplicity of means need not lead to drab expressions where the dull, the conventional and the monotonous exude boredom.

And using simple means, of course, does not entail rejecting certain indispensable means for communicating across the world.

But for the younger generation, what is going to matter is for the Church to lead them to a source from which wonder and astonishment are continually springing up afresh. For the young the Church is recognizable when it is a place where Christians are not trying to survive at all costs, but to be born and reborn. The Church is recognizable when it touches the whole of their being, body and spirit. Then it captivates, then it leads us to take risks, and still more risks, for Christ's sake and the Gospel's, until our dying day.

Go To Meet Those Who Cannot Believe

Now, at the end of the twentieth century, we Christians are confronted with the result of our divisions—mutual impoverishment.

We are surrounded by non-Christians, and also by Christians for whom the faith is a matter of indifference. They can only believe what they see with their own eyes. How can they take us seriously as long as our brotherly love is not plain for all to see?

A time of confrontation is coming. We are all concerned because we are all challenged. After twenty centuries of Christianity, more and more baptized persons are losing interest in the faith. At the same time, in spite of our Christian presence throughout the world, living condition are deteriorating year by year in certain regions of the globe.

Our communion is a function of all these people; it is for them all. We do not desire it for our own happiness, or to be stronger over against

others. We desire it solely in order to follow our vocation to be universal.

We will never encounter those who do not believe unless we are all
together. Not that we are asked to betray the truth! But if we agree on
one basic truth, the necessity of visible communion, we will have found
the existential possibility of agreeing one day on other truths of the
faith.

There is the promise of a new dynamism to those who come together
again after separation. Those who have achieved reconciliation find that
their mind and heart have been opened, and even in old age they renew
their youth. They regain vital energy. In the same way, Christians
throughout the world will experience in the rediscovery of visible communion the youthfulness and vitality of a new springtime.

The dynamic of reconciliation will bring us out of the state of impoverishment brought about by our divisions. Its impetus will allow us to
overcome our inability to join a world which, though it may not expect
much from us, would be justified in expecting everything from men and
women who call themselves Christians.

But the confrontation now in preparation will mean, in the strongest
sense of the word, an awakening for everyone. For all of us, together, to
go and meet those who cannot believe, we are asked to make the secret
offering of our lives day by day.

The real history of the ecumenical movement will never be written.
It lies in the inner faithfulness in things large and small of those whose
whole inner life is engaged in the struggle. For a long time to come
ecumenism will be advancing against the stream of conformity; dialogue with those farthest from us will never happen as a matter of
course.

At Taizé the vocation to ecumenism has made us open, year in and year
out, to all that is human. It has awakened in us an interest in those who
were farthest from us. Without a passion for the unity of the Body of
Christ, we never would have discovered this friendship with so many
people all over the world.

Our concern for dialogue has made us attentive to everything human.
Who would not burn with desire to understand other human beings in
their life struggle: the light that has gone from their eyes or the hard-
won serenity, the whole personality held in check, the scars of conflict-

ing impulses, the generous gift of themselves or the firm will to keep themselves back.

The spirit of mercy disposes the heart of stone to become a heart of flesh. It leads to a strong love, devoid of sentimentality, that caricature of tenderness. It refuses to turn the spotlight on one's self. It invites us to accept in quiet trust our neighbor, whoever he or she may be, and any event whatsoever.

Why is it that, although they say they know God, so many Christians behave as if they had never found him? They show no mercy. They profess the God of Jesus Christ and yet their hearts remain hard.

On the other hand, why is it that so many agnostics, in the wake of the publicans and tax collectors, "are entering the Kingdom ahead of us"? They open up a way of peace, they are men and women of communion, and they often show greater concern for peacemaking than many Christians do.

It is possible to believe that people of this kind are unconsciously bearers of Christ, although they have no explicit faith. Could this not be the result of the prayers of so many Christians throughout the ages? People hear God's voice without recognizing him; they are obedient to him and they live lives of charity. How can we avoid applying the words of Christ to them: "They go before us into the Kingdom"? They open doors for us; they clear the way.

There are many who profess to love Christ but do not know him. And there are many who love him, although they claim that they do not know him.

There are many who are children of light unawares. In any case they are easy to recognize: full of concern for their neighbors, they flee the works of darkness, all that is murky and lacking in transparence.

Dialogue with someone who does not believe sometimes allows us to discover in such persons what they do not recognize by themselves, the mystery of a hidden presence.

Only someone whose life is animated at all times by the Word of God and the Eucharist can speak like this, of course. Otherwise the result would be relativism, which does nobody any good. To say that there are people who follow God without knowing him could constitute an invitation to cease all commitment for Christ. What then would be the good of praying, or of remaining in God's presence?

A Way Out Of A Dead End

IN THESE YEARS when contemporary societies are moving from one crisis to another at an ever more rapid rate, Christians too are being shaken. They are experiencing the subtle sickness of disintegration.

At a time when the ever growing number of people with no knowledge of God staggers the mind, the weight of Christian disunity is a heavy burden to bear.

When Christians are imprisoned in parallel confessions with their rivalries and competition, the best in each of them is neutralized. And sadness remains.

A saying of Jesus is becoming relevant as never before: when you are bringing your gift to the altar and someone has something against you, leave everything, first go and be reconciled.

"First go." Not "put it off till later."

Does not the noble ecumenical vocation need to be transfigured by the miracle of a reconciliation not put off until later?

We are beyond the pioneering stage. To heal old wounds, and more recent ones, it is imperative for the ecumenical vocation to turn a new corner. It has been able to create remarkable organizations for dialogue, as well as many commissions and research groups. In order to turn the next corner, it is essential for all its resources, its structures and its spiritual insights to be transfigured into the ability to effect reconciliation here and now.

To remain no longer on parallel paths, not to look back, to forgive each other—that is the heart of the matter.

On the eve of the Second Vatican Council, the splendid hope of a speedy reconciliation between the non-Catholic churches and the Church of Rome was born. In the years following, the spirit of unity fostered new understanding and friendships. Since that time, remarkable theological documents have been drawn up.

But as time passed, it became clear that a reconciliation between the non-Catholic churches and the Church of Rome seemed to be relegated to a more or less distant future.

Those who longed for this reconciliation are perhaps more numerous than is generally supposed. And there are many who pursue painstaking theological research and dialogues of all kinds at the instigation of ecumenical institutions. Nevertheless the weight of history, which has created a kind of unconscious intransigeance, still remains.

In the face of serious impossibilities, what is the good of having illusory hopes or of encouraging God's People to hold them?

God condemns no one to immobility. He never closes the ways ahead. God is always offering new ones, even if they are sometimes narrow. So the question arises: How to find a way out of a dead end? Where can we find a road to immediate reconciliation, even the smallest way possible, for a time of transition?

Such a way exists. It is not an easy way out. It does not consist in a watering down of the faith, since it always presupposes the same faith, the same thinking and the same hope.

This little way forward can be only a personal one, an inner way. It is the way of reconciliation within oneself, in one's own being.

Without humiliating anybody, without becoming a symbol of repudiation for anyone, we can welcome within ourselves the attentiveness to the Word of God, so dearly loved by the Church families born of the Reformation, together with the treasures of spirituality of the Orthodox churches, and all the charisma of communion of the Catholic Church, in this way disposing ourselves day after day to put our trust in the mystery of the faith.

In the course of many centuries since the Church began, since Mary and the apostles, the motherhood of the Church was one. This is still true today. It does not cease to be the case when, at a given moment, divisions occur.

As ecumenism has advanced, could it be that an evolution has been partially stifled as a result of the conspiracy of silence maintained around the ministry of the Pope? Can ecumenism ever move forward if no appeal is made to a pastoral ministry of unanimity, on a worldwide scale? And in a very concrete fashion, because we are human beings with ears to hear and eyes to see.

A man named John made me move toward these perspectives. John XXIII, by his ministry, opened my eyes to this path of universality. As contemporaries of this witness to Christ, we remain challenged by him.

During the last conversation I had with Pope John XXIII, shortly before he died, I sensed that his prophetic ministry had been refused and that, as a result, a turning point of ecumenism had been missed. He had reversed the situation of Counter-Reformation, among other things by declaring publicly, "We will not put history on trial; we will not ask who was wrong and who was right." He had taken huge risks. At the Second Vatican Council, going against the advice of many, he had not hesitated to invite non-Catholics. He had asked forgiveness for the past. He was ready to go a long way. I realized his hurt on receiving in return, from non-Catholics, nothing but polite words. During that last conversation I understood that a prophet had been rejected, that ears had been stopped. From that moment on ecumenism would sink down into a system of parallel roads, with each denomination pursuing its separate course in simple peaceful coexistence, nothing more.

If it is true that every local community needs a pastor to renew the communion between people ever inclined to scatter, how can there be hope of a visible communion between all the Christians of the whole world without a universal pastor? Not at the top of a pyramid, not at the head (Christ is the head of the Church), but at the heart.

As universal pastor, is the Bishop of Rome leading us toward a Church of communion, not looking for support to any economic or political powers? If so, then he, supported by his local Church, is going to count for much in the search to promote a communion among all.

What can we ask of such a pastor, called to live as a poor bishop? Surely, to expound the sources of faith for each generation, and, in just a few words, to invite Christians—and also many people beyond the borders of the Church—to struggle against oppression and injustice.

Of course the Bishop of Rome is weighed down with an enormous burden of history, which at present still makes it hard to glimpse the specific features of his vocation. Today he is called to rid himself of local pressures in order to be as universal as possible, in order to be free to express prophetic intuitions. And free as well to exercise an ecumenical ministry which fosters communion between all the churches, even calling on those that refuse his ministry.

Perhaps the "servant of the servants of God" has a responsibility not just for Catholics, but for non-Catholics too. Is it not, in a word, to confirm his brothers, so that they may be of one faith and of one mind? "Peter, confirm your brothers."

By writing these lines I may have hurt someone, or hung a stone about his neck. Then let him hang that stone, too heavy for him, around my own neck. Not that I pretend to be able to bear it, but at least I shall try.

Reawakened From Within

HOW OFTEN, in the daily dialogues with young people from different countries, does the same question come up: "Why do you love the Church; its structures hurt us so much?"

Should those who at times suffer from the Church run away from her? But is not running away from the Body of Christ bound to lead to abandoning the Risen Christ on the roadside? Remaining within, with infinite courage, is not that the way to transform rigid structures?

A first-century Christian had grasped that a fundamental reality—which, in the end, sets everything in motion—was communion in the Body of Christ. "The reality is the Body of Christ," writes Paul to the Colossians, "and let no one try to deprive you of it."

Why do we love this communion to such a degree? When it is radiant, it makes visible Christ's own face. It does not exist for believers only, but for all human beings. It is a communion within which kindness and the spirit of mercy are born, and through which are stimulated not only hope rooted in Christ, but also a fine human hope.

Over the past few years, in modern-day societies that are becoming more and more anonymous, many little groups of Christians have sprung up. They are a kind of antidote to a secularized world. With the freshness of the Gospel, these groups bridge a gap between faith and life. Forms of commitment adapted to a rapidly changing world are discovered in them.

A quality of extreme fragility is an inevitable feature of these little communities because of the provisional nature of their life. In order to survive, some of them turn into exclusive little circles with positions which cut them off on all sides. Provided a few feel that they get along well together, they are ready to jump on any bandwagon, however esoteric its form. When Christians are fragmented into such tiny particles, what happens to communion in the Body of Christ?

Elsewhere, the large communities called "parishes" do not exactly engender enthusiasm. On our travels across the continents, we cannot help but notice that the great majority of Christians normally meet for worship in these large local communities. But the young are ill at ease in them when their aspirations are not recognized and they find no scope for their energies. They are bored in the churches, and boredom is spiritual suffering.

Might we not be in a period of new birth and growth regarding common prayer? If the abundance of words in churches is a cause of fatigue, we will soon be obliged to have more and more singing in our prayer.

If young people found they could join in the Eucharist, at least every Sunday, and continue the prayer by staying in church and singing, they would already be creating a space of worship.

Letter To Religious Communities

Introduction

In creating a common life at Taizé, our sole desire was to be a family of brothers committed to following Christ, as an existential sign of the communion of the People of God.

A life in community is a living microcosm of the Church, an image on a small scale containing the whole reality of the People of God. And so the humble sign of a community can find a resonance far beyond the limitations of the individuals who make it up.

The world of today needs images more than ideas. No idea can be accepted unless it is clothed in visible reality, otherwise it is only ideology. However weak the sign, it takes on its full value when it is a living reality.

To live out our ecumenical vocation authentically, we must be deeply concerned to realize a communion in our life together. The fact that some of us belong to different Reformation churches or to the Anglican Communion, and that it is possible to have Catholic brothers as well, does not in any way put up barriers between us. The communion of faith is forged through liturgical prayer, and takes shape slowly.

We know that we are not in a privileged situation, for our combat is intense. But if we had to start all over again, we would not hesitate.

With the great freedom given by our situation, we might well have taken no account of those who preceded us in the common life. But what sort of a life would that have been, lived outside of all solidarity? Being attentive to the mystery of the People of God has led us to consider that Taizé is only a simple bud grafted on a great tree, without which it could not survive.

In this regard it is undoubtedly significant that our village lies between Cluny and Citeaux.

On the one hand Cluny, the great Benedictine tradition which humanized everything it touched. Cluny, with its sense of moderation, of visible community built up in unity. Cluny, the center of attraction for men consciously or unconsciously seeking their own inner unity and unity with their neighbors.

Among the abbots of Cluny is the figure of that outstanding Christian, Peter the Venerable, so human, so concerned for charity and for unity, capable of gestures centuries ahead of his time. So it was that when two popes had been elected by the conclave, he was magnanimous enough to ask the one who belonged to Cluny, one of his own brothers, to step down for the sake of unity.

In advance of the thinking of his time, he welcomed and offered shelter to Abelard, a man public opinion had condemned.

At that period of history it was he, once more, who inspired his contemporaries by announcing in words of fire the power of a personal encounter:

"Jesus will always be with me, and he will never turn away from
me at any time. Certainly not at any time, for, despising and rejecting all that is not he, I will attach myself to him alone. Jesus will
be my life, my food, my rest, my joy. He will be for me my country
and my glory. Jesus will be everything for me: here below as far as
possible, in hope and love until the gate of eternity: then I shall see
him face to face. He has promised."

On the other hand there is Citeaux, revitalized in Peter the Venerable's time by another Christian no less remarkable: Saint Bernard.
Saint Bernard foreshadows all the reforming zeal which was to explode in the sixteenth century. He renewed Citeaux to reform the Rule
by which Cluny lived. He refused to compromise the absolute of the
Gospel in any way. He spoke the language of a Reformer. He was more
concerned with the demands of the present moment than with historical
continuity. To one of his brothers he wrote:

"There is nothing stable in this world . . . and so, of necessity,
we must either go forward or go back. To remain in the state one
has reached is impossible. Anyone unwilling to advance retreats. It
is Jesus Christ who is the prize of the race. If you stop when he is
striding on, you not only come no closer to the goal, but the goal
itself retreats from you."

Fusing the sense of urgency with a sense of the continuity assured by
several generations is an incomparable factor making for inner peace
and humility: I am a useless servant; what I do not accomplish myself,
others will accomplish after me. From what is now still immature, others
will be able to gather the ripe fruit.

Called to the same vocation, we are thankful to you for having remained faithful, along with those who have gone before you, to the
great call of the Gospel: "Leave everything behind and receive a hundredfold here on earth, together with persecutions."
  By the witness of your community life, which so often has called forth
the reaction "See how they love one another," by your obedience to
God manifested in the humble fidelity of everyday life, by the continuity of your worship across the centuries, and by so many other

values, maintained throughout the ages, you are a support for us and a cause for hope.

In a great diversity of spiritual families, you have maintained a unity necessary for the building up of the Body of Christ. By this witness of unity, as well as by the gift of your lives, renewed day after day, you encourage us to run in the very footsteps of Christ.

And now some of you, along with men committed to the priesthood, want to discover in our life a confirmation of the call to chastity that they received from Christ: "Leave everything behind and receive a hundredfold here on earth, together with persecutions." It is true that if a solidarity exists, it does indeed lie in the common combat to live authentically that mysterious call from Christ.

God names ambassadors of Christ, in spite of the limits of their lives as human beings, those who answer him with the yes and the Amen of a faithful heart.

To those who have accepted not to begin a family according to the flesh, God gives an openness of heart and mind to love every human and spiritual family. Those who, for the sake of Christ and the Gospel, open their arms to all, no longer closing them on anyone and not seeking to possess exclusively any other person, are able to have a universal, authentically catholic outlook, and as a result to understand every human situation. Those who, in their search for God, have chosen Christ as their first love, are enabled to ensure a hidden presence of Christ in the midst of people who cannot believe.

Some have told me that at Taizé, the common life, purified of a weight of traditions, is lived in its first freshness better than elsewhere.

If we made this claim, we would be contradicting our vocation to Christian unity. Our existence would imply a judgment that would be no less harsh for being implicit. We would then be protesters, and thus locked into a posture of self-sufficient complacency. The road to unity does not involve protest. Those who want to criticize the faults of others from without can only imprison them in themselves.

When we are told of this or that unfortunate situation weighing upon one of your institutions, we keep silent, since we know that judgments from the outside have always led to the hardening of positions. When you suffer, we love you all the more for it. And if we are given the opportunity to say what we think, we only do so when we are sure it will not foster a spirit of rebellion, so that "the peace of Christ, to which we have been called in order to form one body, may reign in our hearts."

And now, some of you no longer wish to remain in solidarity with your brothers and sisters in the difficult journey of a vocation. Some prefer to call their commitment into question, with the risk of destroying the unity of the personality. But this unity cannot be taken apart with impunity. Others threaten. But a body, no matter how small, can never be reformed by threats of division. It is always from within, and with infinite patience, that new life can be reawakened when it is needed. Only then can a confrontation be creative. Any break that at first seems to reduce tensions is in the final analysis an impoverishment. It is a refusal to take the costly steps forward necessary to any life in God that is fully responsible and in solidarity with others.

Those threatened by discouragement should know this: today more than ever, when it is charged with the life-force proper to it, when it is filled with the freshness of brotherly love which is its distinctive feature, community life is like yeast at work in the dough of Church and world. It can raise mountains of apathy and bring people an irreplaceable quality of the presence of Christ.

Community life contains a force of openness to other men and women. It would be possible, of course, to withdraw into ourselves and to turn away from our neighbors, since the contemplative life orients us toward the inner world. But what fires us in our depths is our fellow human beings, their promotion in God as well as their human promotion. What keeps us going deep down is to live Christ for the world. And since as time passes it is necessary for us to go back to the essential lines of our vocation, one of the elements of this "second conversion" lies in the answer we give to the question: Who is my neighbor?

But if, on account of our generous openness to other people, signs of the intemporal were to disappear from our life, we would have acquired only a particular ability to share in the lives of our contemporaries. We would stop at a dimension that nonbelievers can attain equally well. And, on the other hand, we would be unable to allow people to glimpse the event of God and his transcendence. In pluralistic, secularized societies, what is needed more than ever are places where transcendence becomes more perceptible, where the city of God joins the city of man. Today we find our place where the vertical line of God encounters the human community.

If the world, swept by the great currents of contemporary history, makes itself felt even in the depths of our being, if the monastic vocation is more exposed than ever before because it is prey to the powerful tensions and attractions of our day, then the call of Christ remains all the more urgent.

Because of all that you are, brothers and sisters living the religious life, we sing the joy of our common vocation to God the Father, to his Son Jesus Christ, to the Holy Spirit, asking by the offering of our lives the grace of the visible unity of all in the same Church.

United to you in the joyous communion of all the saints of Christ, waiting for him to transfigure in us all that is opposed to our vocation, we express our gratitude for all you have been and all that you are.

At The Heart Of The Church
(Letter To Catholics Confronting One Another)

BEING CATHOLIC MEANS bearing a commitment. Catholic, ecumenical and universal are synonyms.

A universal solidarity among all the people on earth is more necessary than ever. Without it, there can be no hope for peace on earth, nor for the human and economic promotion of the poorest.

Being Catholic means being open to all the concerns of people today.

And now, Catholics are beginning to confront one another. We are afraid the necessary confrontation between Catholics will turn into opposition.

Who would deny that confrontation can be necessary? In a dialogue that touches the real questions, it becomes possible for each participant to understand the others' attitudes, the reasons for their choices. Only such a frank encounter enables us to grasp the basic motivations behind this or that tendency. Aware of the forces of secularization that influence Christians as never before, some have received a mission to awaken others to a sense of the sacred, to the veneration of the mystery of the Church, to the need for an authority as a factor for unity. Others want rather to go as far as possible to encounter people who, in our day, cannot believe.

Confrontation presupposes lucidity and a forceful analysis. But tensions subside if we all go beyond our own particular outlook to understand what the Spirit is saying to the Church through calls other than our own. A dialogue becomes richer when each participant makes an effort to understand the calls that are addressed to their Catholic brothers and sisters who have a different mission, but who are deeply committed to serving the *Catholica,* the community of baptized persons spread across the earth.

The diversity of tendencies is a guarantee of freedom as well as a stimulant making for fruitful dialogue. But when confrontation loses sight of its purpose, when a concern for the entire body disappears, then each person is tempted to withdraw to one side of the fence, the "right side," and to criticize those who have a different mission, marking them with a label.

As a consequence, some may find no course open to them but to dig in their heels and come to a standstill, while others, in the name of reforms, are in danger of running around in circles, in the end calling everything into question, even the very foundations, in the belief that the most extreme positions are the most worthwhile.

When some say that, no matter how violent the oppositions between Catholics may become, the age of schisms is past—and I am fully convinced of that—I join many others in replying: if on one side things come to a complete standstill, and on the other every institution is called into question, are not many who see this going to become indifferent to our fundamental vocation to unity?

In the eyes of so many people, an essential vocation of the Catholic Church in our day is to live out her unity. This internal unity is necessary to prepare together the communion, the visible unity of all Christians, the only basis for us to encounter men and women who are unable to believe.

Without a restored unity, there will be no place where a disinterested encounter will be open to all. In the One Church, the love of Christ consumes each person with the fire of charity.

Today is a time of intense combat. Within our church communities, we are challenged by contradictory voices, and from without, a host of ideas and images affects every Christian, even the most protected.

To remain unshaken, to move forward beyond our own limitations, to see beyond immediate issues the essentials common to all, we have to respond to the call to holiness, lived not by the lukewarm but by beings of flesh and blood, transfigured by Christ, humanized by the Gospel.

FOUR

TRUSTING

Happy Are They Who Die For Love

Never a pause, O Christ, in your persistent questioning: "Who do you say that I am?"

You are the one who loves me into endless life.

You open up the way of risk. You go ahead of me along the way of holiness, where happy are they who die of love, where the ultimate response is martyrdom.

Day by day you transfigure the "No" in me into "Yes." You ask me, not for a few scraps, but for the whole of my existence.

You are the one who prays in me day and night. My stammerings are prayer: simply calling you by your name, Jesus, fills our communion to the full.

You are the one who, every morning, slips on my finger the ring of the prodigal son, the ring of festival.

So why have I wavered so long? Have I "exchanged the glory of God for something useless; have I left the spring of living water to build myself cracked cisterns that hold nothing?" (Jeremiah 2)

You have been seeking me unwearyingly. Why did I hesitate once again, asking for time to deal with my own affairs? Once I had set my hand to the plough, why did I look back? Without realizing it, I was making myself unfit to follow you.

Yet, though I had never seen you, I loved you.

You kept on saying: live the little bit of the Gospel you have grasped. Proclaim my life. Light fire on the earth . . . You, follow me . . .

Until one day I understood: you were asking me to commit myself to the point of no return.

The Wonder Of A Love

Christ Never Forces Anyone's Hand

You keep on asking me, "How can I find fulfillment?"

If only I could lay my hand on your shoulder and go with you along the way.

Both of us together, turning toward Him who, recognized or not, is your quiet companion, someone who never imposes himself.

Will you let him plant a source of refreshment deep within you? Or will you be so filled with shame that you say, "I am not good enough to have you near me"?

What fascinates in God is his humility. He never punishes, never domineers nor wounds human dignity. Any authoritarian gesture on our part disfigures his face and repels.

As for Christ, "poor and humble of heart"—he never forces anyone's hand.

If he forced himself upon you, I would not be inviting you to follow him.

In the silence of the heart, tirelessly he whispers to each of us, "Don't be afraid; I am here."

Dying and Rising with Jesus

To joy he calls us, not to gloom.

No groaning at the bonds that bind you, or the tyranny of a self you want to preserve. No drawing back into yourself, intent on mere survival, but at every stage in life, a new birth.

His joy not for your private possession, or all happiness would flee.

I would like to help you make your life a poem of love with him. Not a facile poem, but through the very grayness of your days, his joyfulness, even hilarity. Without them, how could there be fulfillment?

Whatever your doubts or your faith, he has already placed ahead of you what fires your enthusiasm.

Nobody can answer for you. You and you alone must dare.

But how?

Go to the ends of the earth and plunge into the conditions of those society rejects; overturn the powers of injustice; restore human dignity: Is that taking risks? Yes, but that's not all there is to life.

Or again: Sharing all you own, could that be the risk of the Gospel?

As you try to follow Christ, the day will come when you are irresistibly drawn to that. Responding will mean drinking deep at the unfailing springs. Anyone refusing to quench his thirst there first would become, unconsciously, a doctrinaire of sharing.

But what is the greatest risk to which this Man of humble heart invites everyone? It is "dying and rising with Jesus."

Passing with him from life to death; at times accompanying him in his agony for all the human family and, each day anew, beginning to rise from the dead with him.

Joyful, not overwhelmed. Every moment, leaving everything with him, even your weary body. And using no exotic methods, for then you would have lost the sense of praying.

Will you be able to wait for him when your heart cries out in loneliness, and the ultimate question is torn from your soul: "But where is God?"

Wait for him, even when body and spirit are dry and parched. Wait, too, with many others for an event to occur in our present day. An event which is neither marvel nor myth, nor a projection of yourself. The fruit of prayerful waiting, it comes concretely in the wake of a miracle from God.

In prayer, prayer that is always poor, like lightning rending the night, you will discover his secret: you can find fulfillment only in the presence of God . . . and also, you will awaken others to God, first and foremost, by the life you live.

With burning patience, don't worry that you can't pray well. Surely you know that any spiritual pretension is death to the soul before you begin.

Even when you cannot recognize him, will you stay close to him in long silences when nothing seems to be happening? There, with him, life's most significant decisions take shape. There the recurring "What's the use?" and the scepticism of the disillusioned melt away.

Tell him everything, and let him sing within you the radiant gift of life. Tell him everything, even what cannot be expressed and what is absurd.

When you understand so little of his language, talk to him about it.

In your struggles, he brings a few words, an intuition or an image to your mind . . . And within you grows a desert flower, a flower of delight.

The Fire of His Forgiveness

Fulfillment? I would like to clear you a path to the springs of living water. There and nowhere else, imagination and the potent energies of risk blossom and flourish.

Don't you see? In every human being, a gift that is unique. Everything exists to a greater or lesser degree within you, every possible tendency. In you fertile fields, in you scorched deserts.

Fulfillment? Don't count yourself among those who have made it. You would lose vital energies, and the transfiguration of the will into creative potential.

No self-indulgence. Don't waste time in dead-end situations. Move on, unhesitating, to the essential step, and quickly.

Unconsciously, you may wound what you touch. Only Christ can touch without wounding.

Consider your neighbors not just in one stage of their life, but in all its phases. So don't try to separate the weeds from the wheat. You will only uproot them both and leave devastation behind you, exchanging the gleaming pearl for cracked earth that cannot hold water.

But you say, "How can I fulfill myself when there is an image from my past which covers the spring of living water in ashes? . . . Forget the ravages of the past? Nobody can do that; nor the still throbbing pangs of clinging regret."

But let just one sigh rise from deep within you, and already you are overflowing with confidence. What holds you in its clutches is being dealt with by God.

For you, this prayer: "Forgive them, they don't know what they are doing; forgive me, I didn't know what I was doing."

"Love!" It's easily said. Forgiving means loving to the utmost . . . Forgive not in order to change the other person but solely to follow Christ. No one can come closer to the living God than that . . . And you yourself become a source of forgiveness.

In times of darkness, when life loses its meaning and you are unsure even of your own identity, a flame still burns bright enough to lighten your night . . .

. . . The fire of his forgiveness plunges deep within you, dispelling your own confusion; he calls you by your name; and the fire burns away your bitterness to its very roots. That fire never says "enough."

Become What You Are

Fulfillment? Could you be hesitating over a choice for fear of making a mistake? Bogged down perhaps in the mire of indecision?

The fact is, a "Yes" to Christ for life is surrounded by an element of error; but this is already purified, from the start, by an act of faith. So set out unseeing, taking him at his word.

Don't summon your own darkness again to cover your refusal. Happy all who tear their hand from their eyes to take the greatest of all risks, "dying and rising with Christ."

Fulfillment? Become what you are in your heart of hearts . . .

. . . and the gates of childhood will open, the wonder of a love.

All Or Nothing

YOU ASPIRE TO follow the Risen Christ: How can you know that you have encountered him?

Rather than trying to feel his presence, will you be able to discern God in the simple events of life, and put into practice every day the suggestions he places in you?

What is the sign that you have encountered Christ? When you are led, irresistibly, to leave everything behind, to leave yourself behind, not knowing where you are heading. You have encountered him when, try as you may to stop your ears, within you his words ring out: "You, come and follow me."

Already long before Christ's coming, a believer of the Old Testament wrote: "You wish to serve the Lord, prepare yourself for trials. Be transparent of heart and steadfast." (Sirach 2.1f)

All or Nothing

Choosing Christ is a matter of all or nothing; there is no middle ground. Will you go to the point of bearing in your body the marks of Jesus and the burning of his love? They become visible in you when you are able to tell him: "You loved me first. You are my joy, my essential love—may that be enough for me."

If you wish to follow Christ to the very end, no matter what the cost, prepare yourself, in the poverty of your life, to know times of struggle: the fidelities of daily life which, through simple, ordinary acts, link you to an immense reality. And in you is formed a humanity permeated with understanding for everyone, a heart wide as the world.

By what other sign can you recognize that you have encountered the Risen Lord? When the inner struggles you wage in order to follow him, the trials which can even cause floods of tears to flow within, when this whole combat, far from making you hard and bitter, is transfigured and becomes a source of new energy.

Such a transfiguration is the beginning of the resurrection, already here on earth. It is an inner revolution, the passover with Jesus, a continual passing from death to life.

In this inner revolution, all that could devastate your being—loneliness, loss of meaning, feelings of uselessness—everything that otherwise would shatter the fibers of your soul, all these things no longer block the way forward, but instead lead to a breakthrough from anguish to confident trust, from resignation to creative enthusiasm.

You aspire to follow the Lord, so do not be afraid of entering a passover with Christ. If you do not stop your ears when you hear him say "Come, follow me," you will be surprised to find yourself answering:

"I have recognized you, and so I want to stay close beside you as you listen to the simple words I stammer in prayer—you, the Christ of glory, risen within all who are searching for you. I also want to be able to accompany you in your agony for humankind, since you stay close beside anyone who is in distress, anyone who is struggling on behalf of many others. To put my trust in you, to acquire a steadfast heart, I will go to the point of gathering up all my energies and, violently if need be, go so far as to anchor my heart to God's heart, for I have understood: only the violent take hold of the realities of the Kingdom of heaven."

A life based solely on the confidence Christ places in us is love at its purest, not an illusory love which is content with words, but trust flowing from a love which constantly takes hold of the whole being, a love strong as death.

The Risk of Living

You aspire to follow Christ: you can only encounter him by placing your trust in him; there is no other way.

But how can you trust him and follow him in a lifelong commitment when you are so afraid of making a mistake or, later on, of having made a mistake?

To prepare yourself to say this "Yes," and then to live it, you need to have someone to talk to about yourself. And not just anybody—for then you would look for someone who follows your line of least resistance, and you would never become a creator that way. You can speak about what lies buried in your heart only to someone who has the gift of discernment and is experienced, who can read what lies beneath the contradictions of the personality.

The person who exercises this ministry has no method, no theory. He or she does not give the same answer to everyone—it all depends on each one's basic gift.

To one person he will have to say: "Leave everything right away; otherwise you will be running away from God." To someone else, just as eager to follow Christ, he will say instead: "To commit your whole life to God, first gain the necessary qualifications in a profession, to prepare yourself to serve others. Interrupting your professional training now would be taking the easy way out."

To all, in any case, he will express this certainty: "You will only know God by taking the risk to root your life in him, in a life that is exposed, not protected or withdrawn. And not just for a while but for your entire lifetime. Dare to take this risk over and over again."

The fear of making a mistake is present in youth but it can also return much later. Some people begin to flame in their middle years, thinking they have finally discovered the love of their life. They emphasize the errors that surrounded the decision they made when they were young, forgetting that no action on this earth is absolutely pure, otherwise we would be angels.

When the yes to Christ has been confirmed by the person who has known how to listen to you, go ahead. If you remain in the quagmire of hesitations or regrets, you are wasting your time, time that no longer belongs to you—it is God's now. The portion of error or ambiguity that surrounds every decision will be consumed by the fire of God's Spirit.

You aspire to live dangerously for the sake of Christ, and so every day you will ask yourself the meaning of his words: "Whoever wants to save his life will lose it." And one day, you will understand what this absolute means.

How will you come to understand? Search. Seek and you will find.

Letter To Those Who Think They Have Achieved Nothing

SO MANY WOMEN and men advancing in years think that they have been nothing, that they have achieved nothing worthwhile. They no longer earn their daily bread and they are faced with a desert of loneliness, as if the only thing left for them was to await death.

You who have reached retirement age, do you realize that when it comes to following Christ there is no age for retiring? The time can now begin for the blossoming forth of the gifts of apostolate which have been placed, to a greater or lesser extent, in every baptized person.

There are women and men advancing in years who have known how to love and how to suffer. They have become capable of listening to others and understanding a lot of their struggles. And God gives us all someone or several people to listen to, not for us to give them advice but to go with them to the wellsprings of the living God. For some of you, physical frailty makes it impossible to accompany others except by faithful prayer, and that is of infinite value.

By offering your trust, in particular to members of the younger generations, you respond to the needs of many young people who have been overwhelmed by the upheavals in society, hurt by broken bonds of affection, or left desolate by abandonments.

Using the intuition gained throughout your life, you will uncover paths of trust. Until your very last breath, all is possible.

How wonderful it would be if people came to kiss your worn hands, you who think that you have been nothing and have achieved nothing, and who, without knowing it, enable the unbroken transmission of Christ across the generations.

Letters To Children And Those Who Know How To Listen To Them

DO YOU KNOW how much each one of you can be a reflection of God for others, for your family, for old people around you?

Could you invite those with whom you live to spend a moment of silence together once a week? During this time, even without saying it aloud, everyone could forgive in their hearts the ways in which the others hurt them. And this way, doors of peace will open for you.

Would you like to ask your parents, or those who take their place, to trace the sign of the cross on your forehead before you go to sleep or when you are going out? Then doors of trust would open for you. Remember, God loves you more than you can imagine.

If you can do a drawing to show "trust on earth" and send it to us, we will share it with other people around the world. And if you can copy

the "Letter to those who think they have achieved nothing" and send it
to Taizé, we will send it on to elderly people in other countries.

If every day were to become like a Christmas night . . .
   While you are still young, you can already be an ambassador of trust
and a person who sows forgiveness.
   Some actions can speak for themselves. For example, when you have
offended someone close to you, will you dare to offer them the palm of
your hand for them to trace out there with their finger the sign of the
cross?
   Many of you have experienced being left abandoned by others. To
those your own age who have been hurt by family breakups, your presence could be so essential.
   Work schedules are sometimes very demanding and leave hardly any
time for people to pray together. Couldn't you then prepare a prayer in
your home for your family?
   As you grow older, you may at times be troubled by what you discover in yourself and in others. It can then be a liberation to confide in
someone who listens, someone who, with the perspective of age, seeks
to listen to you disinterestedly.
   Those of you who with passing years have acquired a spirit of discernment—women and men in all parts of the world—are many in number.
You are able to understand what lies in the heart of a child or a young
person.
   Will you help those to whom you listen to look at themselves, and
others too, in the light of the kindliness with which God loves us?
   If you could only communicate to them a peaceful confidence that the
past is buried in the heart of God and that, day by day, he takes care of
our future.
   If all of us—children, women and men of all ages—tried to live in
this confidence, each day would be lit up like Christmas night.

Accompany Christ By A Simple Life

WITHOUT LOOKING BACK, you want to follow Christ: remember that you cannot walk in Christ's footsteps and at the same time follow yourself. He is the way, a way leading you irresistibly to a simple life, a life of sharing.

The Gospel calls you to leave all things behind. But leaving yourself behind is not a matter of self-destruction; it means choosing God as your first love. Simplifying and sharing does not entail opting for austerity or that self-sufficiency which is a burden on others. Nor does it mean glorifying a harsh and abject poverty.

Simplify in order to live intensely, in the present moment: you will discover the joy of being alive, so closely linked to joy in the living God. Simplify and share as a way of identifying with Christ Jesus, born poor among the poor.

If simplifying your existence were to awaken a guilty conscience because of all you can never achieve, then stop and take the time to think things over: jubilation, not groaning; everything around you should be festive. Use your imagination in arranging the little you have, to bring gaiety to the monotony of your days.

You need so little to live, so little to welcome others. When you open your home, too many possessions are a hindrance rather than a help to communion with others. Wearing yourself out to ensure an easy life for members of your family risks placing them in a relationship of dependence.

Do not worry if you have very little to share—such weak faith, so few belongings. In the sharing of this little, God fills you to overflowing, inexhaustibly.

If A Trusting Heart Were At
The Beginning Of Everything

IN YOUR DARKNESS a fire is being kindled which will never die out.

If you want to carry a fire right into the darkest nights of humanity,*
will you let an inner life grow, deep within you? A life with neither
beginning nor end. A land on fire. Even when hidden under the ashes,
it kindles a flame of passionate expectancy. The most captivating thing
about your existence is the continual unfolding of such a life within.
There lies the most incredible human adventure.

If a trusting heart were at the beginning of everything, if it guided
your every step, big or small, you would go a long way. You would see
people and events, not with anxiety, which cuts you off and which does
not come from God, but with a way of looking that is filled with inner
peace. And then you would become a ferment of trust and peace even
where the human community is torn apart, in its deserts.

Across the earth, so many others, believers and nonbelievers, are
already striving to be a leaven of trust between peoples. Seeking healing for the divisions between South and North, between East and West,
they stand out as signs of what we were hardly daring to hope for.

They are there to be seen. They have drawn strength from times of
incomprehensible trials. They persevere, come what may, despite the
unwillingness around them to move forward.

Every human being experiences deserts of fear. But wherever you
are, Christ murmurs in you: "Let your heart trust. Rest in peace in God
alone. Are you frightened? I am here."

* One of the dark nights of humanity at the moment is the one which covers the deserts of
Africa, where the population of the Sahel, on the southern edge of the Sahara, is suffering
from famine caused by drought. It was suggested to Brother Roger to go there. He went
with two of his brothers to Mauritania, one of the poorest countries of Africa, to be in
contact with those who are suffering, to share whatever possible, and to pray silently.

But, you will say, my work, an atmosphere of doubt, my whole past, all pull me so far away from faith in God.

Faith is not a theory. Even at times when God is incomprehensible, what matters most is not first to understand God, but to give your trust.

The day will come when you will be able to find words to express those glimpses you have caught of the indescribable mystery which is God. You can make out its contours. You know him through Christ Jesus who is God in transparency.

The trust of heart which is drawn from faith does not consist in seeing wonders everywhere, as if it held a magical power.

This trust is often held back deep within you: it needs to rise up through your whole being, to well up from obscurity toward clear awareness.

In everything you do, at every moment, commit yourself to the Holy Spirit, and when you have forgotten, give yourself once again. In the silence of your heart, even in your deserts, the Holy Spirit speaks to you, sometimes in just a single word.

When your hopes are disappointed, would you let yourself be submerged in discouragement and doubt? The Risen Christ is with you. Your trials, the thorns within you, are consumed by his fire; and even the stones in your heart, through Christ, can become glowing coals, a light in the darkness.

When you think yourself unloved and not really understood, Christ Jesus asks you continually: "Do you know that I loved you first? Do you love me?" And you stammer your reply: "I love you, Jesus, perhaps not as I would like to, but I do love you."

A life within. Poetry of the Spirit of God. Fulfillment of your longing.

In all of us there is a spiritual strength which does not come from us. It can be refused or rejected, but it is always there. It is never taken away. It is a wellspring of confident trust planted by the Spirit of the living God. Everything flows from this.

If we were able to fathom the heart, the wonder would be to discover in the depths an expectation, a silent longing of love.

From the depths of the night of humanity a hidden aspiration is arising. Contemporary men and women, caught up in the anonymous rhythms of plans and schedules, have an implicit thirst for the one important reality: an inner life, signs that point to the invisible.

Nothing awakens and refreshes our personal inner life like a full, all-embracing common prayer which is meditative and accessible to all age groups. And the high point of the prayer will be the singing that never ends and that continues within, even when you are alone.

When the mystery of God is revealed by the simple beauty of signs, and not smothered under an excess of words, then a generous common prayer, far from being monotonous and boring, opens us to the joy of God on earth. People come running from all directions to discover what they had been unconsciously lacking.

And the presence of all age groups, from the very oldest down to little children, speaks to us. It helps us to grasp that there is just one human family.

Nearly three thousand years ago, a believer named Elijah had the intuition that God speaks to us in the desert and that a silent trust lies at the beginning of everything.

One day Elijah was called to go to the desert of Mount Sinai to listen to God. A storm arose, then an earthquake, then a raging fire. But Elijah realized that God was not speaking to him in these eruptions of nature.

And perhaps for one of the first times in history this clear insight came to be written down: God does not assert himself by violence, he does not communicate through exterior signs of power that frighten. God is not the author of war, disasters, misery, or any human suffering.

Then everything became calm and Elijah heard God in a quiet murmur. And this striking fact dawned on him: often the voice of God comes in a breath of silence.

Are you aware that God visits you? In a breath of silence, in a whisper, God speaks to you humbly. Simply remaining in silence, in God's presence, to receive the Spirit, is already prayer. God will show you the way. And at times silence can be everything in prayer.

The day will come when you realize, and perhaps will say, "No, God was not far away, but I was absent. He was with me." And times are given when God is everything.

Discover God's peace in inner silence. He gives it in all situations, even in the rush and noise of a crowd or in the most demanding activities.

If a trusting heart were the beginning of everything, you would be ready to dare a "yes" for your whole life.

In the Gospel, Jesus speaks about a son who was called to go and work in a vineyard. He answered, "No, I won't." But later on he came to himself and went. It was "Yes."

Another heard the same call and answered, "I will go," but did not go. His "Yes" disappeared into thin air.

This Gospel story is about pronouncing a very serious yes, a yes to follow Christ for life.

For some, daring to say yes means responding to Christ's call to the fidelity of marriage.

At the present time, when so many families break apart, will you, if you choose marriage, accept the challenge of persevering until your very last breath? Such faithfulness is a reflection of the faithfulness of Christ himself.

So many children have been scarred by abandonments and deeply hurt by separations, to the point of losing the confidence which is essential for life. Family breakups have wounded the innocence of childhood or adolescence in many young people. Since they were unable to trust those who had given them life, their trust in God has become clouded over. Their hearts are desolate.

Nothing tears someone apart more than the severing of bonds of affection. Disappointment follows, and the sceptical question: "What is the use of living?" Without love, does life still have a meaning?

Broken human relationships are the greatest trauma and the deepest wound of our times.

Will you make of your home a "little church of God," a place of welcome, of prayer, of faithfulness, and of compassion for all those who are entrusted to your care?

There are also some whom Christ calls to follow him by the "Yes" of an entire life in celibacy.

When you begin to understand that this "Yes" commits your entire life, you become aware of a great unknown: How can I ever hold true? Who has the inner resources for giving oneself in such a way? First there is hesitation and a "No," in a startled reaction that is almost an integral part of our human condition.

But one day comes the surprise of finding yourself on the way, following Christ: a yes has been placed by God's Spirit in your innermost being, in what is known as the human subconscious.

The young person in the Gospel began by saying no. God, who

never imposes himself, did not force his lips. But the young person understood that his refusal caused an alienation within him. If he said no, he was no longer being consistent with what was inside him, the Spirit of God, who deep within him was saying yes, with the same yes that was in Mary.

By letting this yes rise up from your depths, it is possible for you to say, "I will."

A yes because of Christ leaves you vulnerable. It makes it impossible for you to run away from yourself and from an essential solidarity with others.

This yes keeps you alert. It keeps your eyes open. Could such a yes ever become drowsy or even fall asleep? Could it run away from Christ in the communion of his Body, the Church, which is shaken on all sides, and flee a world riddled with suffering?

This yes for life is fire, and it is a challenge. Let it burn, the fire that never goes out. And the yes flames up within you.

This yes leaves you vulnerable. There is no other way.

Whenever doubts and the silences of God seem to deepen, will you look to discern the desert flower?

If a trusting heart were the beginning of everything . . .

FIVE

A FINE HUMAN HOPE

Struggle And Contemplation

At the present time, Christians cannot afford to lag behind in the rearguard of mankind, where there is so much useless strife. They must at all costs avoid becoming bogged down.

In the struggle for the voice of the voiceless to be heard, Christians find their place—in the very front line.

And at the same time Christians, even though they be plunged in God's silence, sense an underlying truth: this struggle for and with others finds its source in another struggle that is more and more etched in our deepest self, at that point in which no two people are quite alike. There we touch the gates of contemplation.

Struggle, contemplation: two poles between which we are somehow to situate our whole existence?

Leaven Of Hope In The World

NOW, as the twentieth century is drawing to a close, there are people who are caught up in a maelstrom of fear, their creative powers frozen by panic. They let themselves be sucked under.

It is true that the questions which need to be asked in order to achieve peace on earth are so vast and complex that they leave one breathless.

Far from being paralyzed by vertigo, many Christians, and nonbelievers as well, are keenly aware that the midnight hour has struck, and the dawn of an entirely new future lies ahead.

From this they have acquired a sense of urgency. In preparation for turning the corner of history, they are coming to grips with this new civilization: they are a leaven of confidence in the world.

Fear in the face of the spectacular scientific and technical developments? No. Science and technology are able either to build or to destroy; it all depends on the use to which they are put.

Science and technology are so beneficial when they allow us to glimpse the unlimited possibilities created by the human mind. Methods of food production unknown before will provide solutions where endemic hunger reigns. Has not the extraction of protein from seaweed (and soon even from bacteria) already been started, in quantities which can be doubled again in twenty-four hours? Great discoveries are alleviating or curing physical and moral sufferings. A worldwide civilization, based on new communications media, information systems and satellites, is creating a world in which boundaries are no more.

It is essential to know all this in order not to remain passive: an attitude of "What's the use?" destroys the eagerness to acquire skills with the aim of being among those who build.

On the other hand, it is equally true that scientific techniques are

changes taking place all around them. Far from accepting, they merely put up with them; "they sneer and shake their heads."

This holds true for all social groups. So many Christians pass an irrevocable judgment on the young and thus widen the gulf between the generations. But people who grow old with no ties to the rising generations condemn themselves to vegetating. Because of the enormous changes taking place today, more than any previous generation we need to have minds and hearts open to comprehend the important developments of our time.

It is more and more the case that what we learned in our youth nowhere near approaches the levels attained by present-day knowledge. But if we use our minds day by day, they will be constantly renewed and able to adapt to new situations.

With advancing age the mind is enriched, judgment becomes more acute, and the accumulation of experience and knowledge lends an irreplaceable perceptiveness to our reflection: nothing is so valuable as a long life of hard work.

The more we are linked to eternity, the better we dispose ourselves to live, for we know what we are drawing near to. Growing old then means being rejuvenated by everything that comes to us through contemporary developments.

If the older generations have no right to impose themselves to the exclusion of others, neither can the young take advantage of their age. The Christian community is not a copy of civil societies; everybody has a contribution to make. The generation gap goes against the spirit of ecumenism, and each one of us risks losing everything by it: the young because they no longer benefit from the human and spiritual experience their elders have acquired; the not-so-young and the elderly because they are relegated to a situation where they have no life to live, and can only wait passively for their own deaths.

A Thirst for the Real

As I write these pages day by day, my mind is constantly kept awake here at Taizé by dialogues with many very different young people. They all have one common denominator: an intense desire to enter the world of tomorrow by participating in a rebirth of the Christian community.

Any sectarianism leads to a reaction of withdrawal on the part of the young who, refusing all reference to a history which no longer has anything to say to the present, will tend more and more to set them-

selves up in autonomous groups. Unlike their elders, the young will
have nothing more to do with denominational self-justifications.

They will go where there is life. They have been educated in the
disciplines of technology and are eager to turn ideas into realities, so
they will not put up with the delaying tactics of aged institutions much
longer. If we do not discover together new paths toward communion,
many young Christians will continue to search elsewhere and turn to
universalist ideologies or to spirituality without God.

Conscious of their own dynamism, these generations demand authenticity. The hour for concrete gestures has arrived.

It is true that the situation which must be overcome in the next decades is characterized by several centuries of marking time; at one point
all the different groups of Christians, in order to survive, had to consoli-
date their own traditions, even if that meant cutting themselves off from
one another. Marking time hardens and leads unfailingly to disintegration: anyone who stops creating is heading for self-destruction in the
short term or in the long.

The Gospel in Its Original Freshness

The younger generation is asking for new signs. Does the Holy Spirit
only speak through mature men, the wise men that we have perhaps
become? Might he not also speak to the People of God through the
new generations? Will their questions succeed in touching us to the
quick?

At times the young judge church leaders harshly. They feel that
adults have acquired unjustifiable securities, the privileges which go
with institutions, and so they refuse to enter into communication with
them.

They want the Christian community to be uncompromising. They are
revolted by cleverness. They demand a new lifestyle and, if they do not
find it, they prefer to leave the Church and go where they think they see
more simplicity and more sincerity in human relationships.

What is the best that this generation has to say to us? "Give us existential proof that you believe in God, and that your security is truly in
Him. Prove to us that you are living the Gospel in all its original freshness, in a spirit of poverty, in solidarity with all and not only with the
family of your particular Church."

The Gospel in all its freshness? That means a constantly renewed
waiting for God. It means living in the dynamism of the present, continually returning to the sources. It means reconciliation.

In order to recover the original freshness of the Gospel, could we accept a second conversion? The word is inapt, charged with the emotional overtones our forebears sometimes gave it. But we adults, are we afraid of renewals that are all the more difficult because habits formed over the years and human pride run contrary to the spirit of poverty and to authentic waiting? Pride creates a cleavage through which all the freshness of the Gospel trickles away. But if we accept this conversion in its totality, Christ will enter into the depths of our minds and our hearts. He will even penetrate our bodies, so that in turn we will have "bowels of mercy."

Creating Together

Whether they are Catholics or Protestants, the rising generations demand more than reforms: they demand a rebirth of the Christian community. But very often they put the cart before the horse, forgetting that there is no reform of community without reform of the individual. Being must come before doing. Obsessed by the will for reform, we run the risk of forgetting that renewal begins in the depths of ourselves.

To these young people I keep on saying: In the brotherly communion which brings together several generations today in Taizé, we want to listen to the Holy Spirit in you, enlarging our minds, our spirits and our hearts. Ask God for our conversion and we will build together, and together we will say: "Look, Lord, upon your people; consider our brothers and sisters the world over. We have separated; we do not seem to be able to join together in a common creation. Break down our self-sufficiency. Inflame us all with the fire of your love."

And I also say to them: Nobody constructs starting from nothing. The power of the forces that inhabit you can lead you to believe that you are going to rebuild entirely on your own. But the genius of the People of God is to construct with everybody. Do not forget yesterday. Nothing enduring is accomplished unless it is created along with others.

In the common life of the People of God as in every Christian community, including marriage, each individual member plays a part day by day in re-creating the whole body. If one member is dominated by a personal creative passion, and does work without integrating it into the creative work of the community, that person destroys without realizing it.

For people really to live a common life, the aim of all must be to build together. The sign of communion which will then shine out is

more important than the noblest piece of individual effort, worked out
on the fringe of the community.

Our creative work becomes communal as soon as we consider what
God is preparing for us. So many signs are given us today. God is
preparing for us a Christian community which will be a place of communion, offering to the insecure throughout the world a firm base. No
violence will be used to achieve this communion. No one will ever be
required to renounce one's own Church or one's own family. That
would not be creating together. To do so would be to wound love, and
anyone who wounds love is not building up the People of God.

Taking Risks For World Peace

IN THIS AGE when the claims of human rights have come home to our
consciences as never before, the law of "might is right" still rampages
over the earth. Humanity is experiencing violence, rumors of war,
armed conflicts.

In the Gospel, peace bears the weighty name of reconciliation. This
word requires commitment and can take us very far. Being reconciled
means beginning a whole new relationship; it is a springtime of our
being. What is true between individuals goes for nations too. What a
springtime a reconciliation of nations would be, especially between East
and West!

A whole young humanity on both hemispheres is eagerly waiting for
the frontiers that separate peoples to be brought down, and is not afraid
to take risks for world peace. All these young people have certain basic
characteristics:

In their search for peace, they refuse to uphold sacred egoisms,
whether of a continent, a nation, a race or a generation.

They are aware that, among the prerequisites for world peace, the
most urgent is a fair distribution of the goods of the earth among all.
The inequitable distribution of wealth, especially when held by Chris-

tians, is a wound inflicted upon the whole human community. Many ask: How is it possible that Christians, who often come to share spiritual goods, have in general, in the course of their history, managed so rarely to share their material goods?

Among those seeking after greater justice, there are two different aspirations. They are complementary. Some are more inclined to use all their energies to bring immediate help to the victims of injustice. Others are concerned first and foremost with acting upon the causes, the structures which foster injustice.

Young seekers after peace also know that only equal trust shown to all the peoples of the earth, and not just to a few of them, can lead to the healing of the wounds that tear them apart. And so it is essential never to humiliate the members of a nation whose leaders have committed inhuman acts. Essential also is boundless concern for so many men and women who today, as exiles or immigrants, live on foreign soil. If every home were open to somebody of foreign origin, the racial problem would be partially solved.

In order to share material goods better between North and South, to repair breaches between East and West, sincerity of heart is necessary. Who, whether a political leader or not, could appeal for peace and not achieve it within him- or herself? "Be upright of heart and steadfast," wrote Sirach the Sage twenty-two centuries ago.

In the critical situations of our time, many are prepared to anticipate, in their lives, trust between nations. They seek in God the energies to persevere; they commit all their inner and spiritual resources to anticipate peace and reconciliation, not on the surface but in the depths. They know that they are not called to struggle with the weapons of power, but with a heart at peace. They refuse to take up partisan positions.

Peace begins in oneself. But how can we love those who oppress the weak and the poor? And harder still: How can we love our opponents when they profess faith in Christ? God moves us to pray even for those who hate. God is wounded with the innocent.

"Love your enemies, do good to those who hate you, pray for those who malign you." Making one's own these words of the Gospel requires maturity, and also the experience of having crossed inner deserts of our own.

In that ocean underlying human consciousness there is a longing. Day and night, it receives the answer: peace.

A Life We Never Dared Hope For

TOGETHER WITH THE whole People of God, with people from all over the world, you are invited to live a life exceeding all your hopes. On your own, how could you ever experience the radiance of God's presence?

God is too dazzling to be looked upon. He is a God who blinds our sight. It is Christ who channels this consuming fire, and allows God to shine through without dazzling us.

Christ is present, close to each one of us, whether we know him or not. He is so bound up with us that he lives within us, even when we are unaware of him. He is there in secret, a fire burning in the heart, a light in the darkness.

But Christ is also someone other than yourself. He is alive; he stands beyond, ahead of you.

Here is his secret: he loved you first.

That is the meaning of your life: to be loved for ever, loved to all eternity, so that you, in turn, will dare to die for love. Without love, what is the point of living?

From now on, in prayer or in struggle, only one thing is disastrous: the loss of love. Without love, what is the good of believing, or even of giving your body to the flames?

Do you see? Contemplation and struggle arise from the very same source, Christ who is love.

If you pray, it is out of love. If you struggle to restore dignity to the exploited, that too is for love.

Will you agree to set out on this road? At the risk of losing your life for love, will you live Christ for others?

With People All over the World
On our own, what can we do to give the voiceless their say, and to promote a society without class?

With the whole People of God, collectively, it is possible to light a fire on the earth.

One of Christ's questions hits home. When that poor person was hungry, did you recognize me in him? Where were you when I was sharing the life of the utterly destitute? Have you been the oppressor of even one single human being? When I said, "Woe to the rich"—rich in money, or rich in dogmatic certainties—did you prefer the illusions of wealth?

Your struggle cannot be lived out in ideas that fly from pillar to post and never become reality.

Break the oppressions of the poor and the exploited, and to your astonishment you will see signs of resurrection springing up, here and now.

Share all you have for greater justice. Make no one your victim. Brother or sister to all, run to whoever is despised and rejected.

"Love those who hate you. Pray for those who wrong you." In hatred, how could you reflect anything of Christ? "Love your neighbor as yourself." If you hated yourself, what damage that would do!

But as your life has been filled to overflowing, you try to understand everything in others.

The closer you come to communion, the more efforts the tempter will make. To be free of him, sing Christ until you are joyful and serene.

Tensions can be creative. But when your relationship with someone has deteriorated into seething inner contradictions and noncommunication, remember that beyond the desert something else lies waiting.

We judge other people by what we are ourselves, by our own hearts. Remember only the best you have found in others. With words of liberation on your lips, not a mouthful of condemnation, do not waste your energy looking at the speck in your brother's eye.

If you suffer unfair criticism for the sake of Christ, dance and forgive as God has forgiven. You will find that you are free, free beyond compare.

In any disagreement, what is the point in trying to find out who was right and who was wrong?

Have nothing to do with clever diplomacy; aim at transparency of heart; never manipulate the conscience of others, using their anxiety as a lever to force them into your scheme of things.

In every domain, when things are too easy, creativity is low. Poverty of means leads to living intensely, in the joy of the present moment. But joy vanishes if poverty of means leads to austerity or to judging others.

Poverty of means gives birth to a sense of the universal. And the festival begins once more. The festival will never end.

If festival disappeared from our lives . . . If we were to wake up, one fine morning, in a society replete but emptied of all spontaneity . . . If praying became mere words, so secularized that it lost all sense of mystery, leaving no room for the prayer of gesture and posture, for poetry, for emotion or for intuition . . . If we were to lose childlike trust in the Eucharist and the Word of God . . . If, on our gray days, we were to demolish all we had grasped on days of light . . . If we were to decline the joy offered by Him who eight times over declares "Happy" (Matthew 5) . . .

If festival disappears from the Body of Christ, if the Church is a place of retrenchment and not of universal comprehension, in all the world where could we find a place of friendship for the whole of humanity?

We Are Ourselves Only in God's Presence

If you feel no sense of God's presence within you when you pray, why worry? There is no precise dividing line between emptiness and fullness, any more than between doubt and faith, or fear and love.

The essential is always concealed from your own eyes. But that only makes you more eager than ever to progress toward the one reality. Then, gradually, it becomes possible to sense something of the depth and the breadth of a love beyond all comprehension. At that point you touch the gates of contemplation, and there you draw the energy you need for new beginnings, for daring commitments.

Discovering what kind of person you are, with nobody there to understand you, can provoke a sense of shame at being alive, strong enough to lead to self-destruction. At times it makes you feel that you are living under sentence. But, for the Gospel, there is neither "normal" nor "abnormal," only human beings, made in the image of God. Then who could condemn? Jesus prays in you. He offers the liberation of forgiveness to all who live in poverty of heart, so that they, in their turn, may become liberators of others.

In every single one of us there is a place of solitude no human relationship can fill, not even the deepest love between two individuals.

Anyone who does not accept this solitude sooner or later revolts against other people, and against God himself.

And yet you are never alone. Let yourself be plumbed to the depths, and you will realize that everyone is created for a presence. There, in your heart of hearts, in that place where no two people are alike, Christ is waiting for you. And there the unexpected happens.

In a flash, the love of God, the Holy Spirit, streaks through each one of us like lightning in our night. The risen Christ takes hold of you, and he takes over. He takes upon himself everything that is unbearable. It is only later, sometimes much later, that you realize: Christ came, he gave his overflowing life.

The moment your eyes are opened you will say, "My heart was burning within me as he spoke."

Christ does not destroy flesh and blood. In communion with him there is no room for alienation. He does not break what is in us. He has not come to destroy, but to fulfill. When you listen, in the silence of your heart, he transfigures all that troubles you most. When you are shrouded in what you cannot understand, when darkness gathers, his love is a flame. You need only fix your gaze on that lamp burning in the darkness, till day begins to dawn and the sun rises in your heart.

Hope That Invents The World Anew

THERE IS A Life hidden in us, a Life which rouses our hope. It opens a way forward for each person and for all humanity.

Will you focus your attention on it?

Without this hope, anchored at the very heart of your heart, without this road stretched out beyond yourself, you lose any desire to forge ahead.

Not a projection of your own wishes, but a hope which leads you to live in ways which seemed to lie beyond all hope, even in situations with no apparent solution.

Alone before Christ you will have the courage to wait for the course
of history, even at its most ineluctable, to burst wide open.

This hope produces surging creativity, which overturns all the determinisms of injustice, hatred and oppression.

Alone before Another, hope given by him. Hope that invents the
world anew.

When you let your world revolve around yourself, you are plunged
into self-centeredness, all your powers of creation and love dislocated.

To displace this center, and for love to be kindled there, you are
offered the same fire offered to every person in the world—Christ's
Spirit in you.

His impetus, his spontaneity, his inspiration have only to waken for
life to become intense and real.

In the vanguard of the Church, will you be a carrier of living waters?
Will you quench the thirst of all who are searching for the source?

Peace and justice are not served merely by the desire for them. It is
still essential to go to the source and reconcile in oneself struggle and
contemplation.

Could anyone willingly consent to be a mere conformist in prayer,
justice or peace? Could anyone freely let it be said of him, "He talks but
he does not act, says 'Lord, Lord,' but does not do the Lord's will; he
says, 'Justice, justice,' but does not practice it; he says, 'Peace, peace,'
but within there is war"?

Many others as well as yourself are haunted by this question. Fervent
seekers after Christ in contemplation, they pay the price of justice and
of peace with their own lives.

These words, spoken by young Asians, ring in my ears: "In the past,
forms of prayer imported from abroad shaped us in ways that took no
account of our own native genius; now programs of justice worked out
elsewhere are being imported, sometimes several rival ones—from conformist models of prayer to conformist models of justice!"

In prayer and in the search for justice, saying without doing would
make you one of the oppressors.

Never let yourself be trapped in the alternative, either commitment to
the oppressed or the quest for sources.

Not struggle or contemplation, but both together, one springing
from the other.

This radicalism of the Gospel demands too much for you to pass judgment on those who do not understand.

Even if you are not understood, do not stand still. You are the one to take this risk.

A hand to grasp your own, to lead you out along the way? No one can do that for another . . .

Only he who has recognized you already . . .

From Doubt To A Fine Human Hope

IN THE NORTHERN continents, under the surface there is sometimes a fundamental loneliness, people in the most dire dereliction. Europe and North America have their "homes for the dying" just as much as Asia, only they are invisible. There are young people, faced with an uncertain future, who even wonder why they were born. When they no longer see the meaning of life, they let themselves drift downhill until mere survival is the only goal they have left.

How can we come to self-fulfillment in God, surrounded as we are by an all-pervasive doubt? How can we move from doubt to hope in God, or at least, for nonbelievers, from doubt to a fine human hope?

In my journeys to Eastern Europe in recent years I have had the chance to discover that, though the deserts of doubt stretch over the whole northern hemisphere, young Christians in the East perceive them differently from those in the West.

In the East, circumstances lead some of the young Christians—not all of them, of course—to pay more attention than ever to the essential elements of the faith. They find no answer to the doubt around them except in a far-reaching commitment of their lives.

In the West, as far as the quest for God goes, some young people—not all—seem to be driven to prove that they are emancipated. They have so many possibilities as consumers at their disposal, not only of material goods but also of leisure and of culture itself, that they find self-fulfillment only in what captivates them. Dialogue with a view to understanding God sometimes becomes mere chatter about everything under the sun. The most powerful realities of the Gospel are eroded by empty talk. Some of these young people give up the faith in order to be in a solidarity of doubt with nonbelievers. Taking the easy way out like this is not without effect on the growth of an inner life. Such facile procedures dig a ditch where God disappears.

For anyone seeking fulfillment in Christ, the present situation arouses uneasiness. In both East and West, doubt can attack believers as a kind of subtle, invisible persecution, until they may even begin to think that they have been abandoned by God and his Christ.

In a civilization where doubt is all-pervasive, Christians are deeply affected when they hear it said, among other things, that their faith is only a projection of themselves. The world of doubt becomes corrosive through exclusively cerebral analyses which mean death for the heart.

The temptation of doubt puts our trust in God to the test. It can purify as gold is purified by fire. It can also cast a human being down into the bottom of a well. But still there is always a light shining from above. The darkness is never total. It never invades the whole person completely. God is present even in that darkness.

Harrowed by the trial of doubt, all who want to live the Gospel allow themselves to be reborn day after day by the confidence of God. And life finds meaning again.

The meaning of life cannot be drawn from the clouds or from opinions; it is nourished by a confidence. God sends his confidence like a breath of the Spirit falling on every human being.

One of the irreplaceable marks of the Gospel is that God invites human beings to place their confidence in return in a Man who has come out of the grave and is alive. Faith is not an opinion, it is an attitude: the believer welcomes the Risen Lord and so becomes alive, not half dead. Already in the early days of the Church, Irenaeus of Lyons, a Christian of the third generation after Christ—he had known Polycarp, who had himself been a disciple of John the Evangelist— wrote: "The glory of God is a human being fully alive. The life of a human being is the vision of God."

Elsewhere in the world, large numbers of young people, intent on prayer, would like to devote their abilities to some generous undertaking. In the depths of their hearts there is a sense of the universal, an aspiration for solidarity with the whole human family, often with its most deprived members. When opportunities are offered, they come running from everywhere. But when such occasions do not arise, some of them slip into excruciating discouragement, the supreme temptation of our day.

For these young people, the future seems a dead end. They feel that the older generation is ready to give them material goods, pocket money, salaries and unemployment benefits, but not to offer them a share in building up society. Since they take so little part in decision-making for the ongoing life of societies and for peace, as well as for the building up of the Church, they withdraw into themselves. Their abilities waste away in obsessive boredom.

Young people of all the nations of the earth are aspiring to build peace. They are ready to stand together and be a ferment of peace, even in places where the human family is being torn apart, whether in the East, the West, the North or the South.

Are they really aware of it? These young people have all they need to overturn determinisms of hatred, war and violence, to restore courage to those who were at the mercy of a diffuse, subtle doubt, and to replace disenchantment with a fine human hope.

SIX

A LOVE THAT FORGIVES

Struggle With A Reconciled Heart

W ithout looking back, you want to follow Christ: be prepared, in a life of great simplicity, to struggle with a reconciled heart.

Wherever you are placed, do not be afraid of the struggle for the oppressed, whether believers or not. The search for justice calls for a life of concrete solidarity with the very poorest . . . Words alone can become a drug.

Prepare yourself as well, whatever the cost, for that struggle within yourself to remain faithful to Christ until death. This continuity of an entire lifetime will create in you an inner unity enabling you to pass through anything.

Struggling with a reconciled heart means being able to stand firm in the midst of crippling tensions. Far from smothering your energies, this struggle calls on you to gather together all your vital forces.

Your intentions will perhaps be distorted. If you remain unforgiving, if you refuse a reconciliation, what do you reflect of Christ? Without a prayer for your opponent, what darkness within you! If you lose the ability to forgive, you have lost everything.

Alone, you cannot do much for others. Together, in community, animated by the breath of Christ's loving, a way forward opens up leading from aridity to a common creation. And when a community is a ferment of reconciliation in that communion which is the Church, then the impossible becomes possible.

You try to be leaven in the dough, you try to love the Church, and so often you come up against internal divisions that tear apart Christ's Body, his Church. What characterizes those who seek reconciliation is that, following Christ, they wish to fulfill more than to destroy, to understand more than to exhort. At all times they remain within, until the very fragilities of the Church are transfigured.

When divisions and rivalries bring things to a standstill, nothing is more important than setting out to visit and to listen to one another, and to celebrate the paschal mystery together.

When you are afraid of being criticized, in order to protect yourself you may react spontaneously by taking the initiative and criticizing first. Would you make use of the weapon of a guilty conscience, so contrary to the Gospel, to get something from another? Try to understand others with that all-important trust which comes from the heart; the intelligence will catch up later.

Far from lighting short-lived blazes, give your life to the end, and day after day it will become a creation with God. The further you advance in a communion with Christ, the more you are led to find concrete steps to take in your daily life.

Where Can We Draw The Courage?

YOU ARE SEARCHING for God: are you aware that what matters most is the welcome you extend to Christ, the Risen Lord? By his presence, always offered to each person, by his forgiveness, he brings you to life. By placing your confidence in him and by forgiving, you will break out of your inner prisons to dare to commit yourself as a pilgrim of reconciliation, even in the divisions of the Christian family and even in those which tear apart the human family.

Because of Christ we want to do all in our power so that the genera-tions of today are neither plunged into situations where life has no meaning, nor paralyzed by anguish in the face of destructive forces and wars.

Accompanied by Christ, together we will discover the confidence that comes from the heart, the spirit of childhood that opens onto a child-hood of the Church.

To go forward on this road, here are some suggestions.

The Reconciliation of Christians Can Tolerate No Further Delay

In these times of upheaval, when new separations are appearing, the urgency of a vocation to ecumenical, i.e., universal, reconciliation chal-lenges us more than ever.

What captivates us about the reconciliation of Christians is that Christ wants to make that unique communion which is his Church a ferment of reconciliation for the entire human community—and that is not without creative consequences for world peace. And so, in a Church which is a pilgrim Church, always setting out anew, God makes us "ambassadors in Christ's name, by placing in us the message of reconciliation."

Anyone who wants to be a creator of reconciliation cannot waste a minute of time or energy trying to find out who was wrong and who was right. What counts is putting reconciliation into practice immedi-ately, and we will see new life come into being, not only in us, but around us as well.

To move beyond the present period of confrontation between Chris-tians, we cannot ignore those who have outlooks different from our own. And though it is of the utmost importance to understand others in their differences, to remain there would mean coming to a standstill after the very first step. That is not yet reconciliation.

We cannot forget either that we would be participating in segrega-tions if we accepted the formation of a Church of the young, or a Church of a class, or a Church of the poor, or a Church of a race, or a Church of elites, intellectual or other.

Let Yourself Be Accompanied

How can we, at every moment, open our doors to Christ, welcome him even when we withdraw into ourselves?

In an inner pilgrimage lasting an entire lifetime, visit with Christ each of "our own prisons," and we will see some of the walls fall down. In

their place, spaces of freedom will open up. To our surprise, we will
find that a whole universe of torment has evaporated by itself . . . and
even in old age, there will be the discoveries of a creation which is
always brand new. Little by little, Christ fashions in us a heart as wide as
the world.

Whoever sets out with Christ sees a way of liberation open up, the
way that leads from worry to confident trust. In simple repentance of
heart, try to begin over and over again. And be ready to experience
failures, too. Why worry about a flood of inner tears—there will always
be a Noah's ark on the waters to sing the living God!

Forgiving Means Being Born Again

Nicodemus went to visit Jesus at night and learned from him that without being born again no one can see the Kingdom of God. Reconciliation and forgiveness involve nothing less than a new birth.

And so, setting out in order to be reconciled means putting into
practice the most dynamic announcement of Christ—forgiveness.

When timidity prevents you from asking for forgiveness, why not
dare to make a simple gesture that expresses what is in your heart and
does without words: offering your hand so that the other can make in it
the sign of forgiveness, the sign of the cross?

Children and "Those Who Resemble Them"

Wherever there is simple confidence, the gates of the Kingdom open,
and one day those gates will be called "Praise."

Children can make little pilgrimages by going to visit elderly people,
to find in them a heart filled with confidence—later they will be able to
share this confidence with those around them.

There are children marked for life by a trial. Of them it is possible to
say that, in God's eyes, they are sacred because of the wounded innocence of their childhood. There are those on whom their parents' separation weighs heavily. There are others who, in some urban areas, are
left to fend for themselves; often they do not know where to go to find
a minimum of confidence and a portion of human happiness. Who will
join them to discover with them the same interests: a book, a story, a
game, a personal conversation?

There is also the abyss of loneliness experienced by those who, in
their old age, end their lives with no one around them. Who will go to
fill those hearts thirsting for confidence?

For adults, times have changed so much that it can sometimes be impossible for them to grasp current developments. Is it not up to the younger generations, then, to be the first to try and understand?

In their heart of hearts, do not adults wish to place their confidence in the young? And that confidence is rarely disappointed if, referring to their own youth, older people remember how much they needed to be listened to and understood.

In Search of a "Childhood of the Church"

Turning together toward a childhood of the Church in the present day means opening ourselves to the spirit of childhood: heartfelt confidence, simplicity, the wonder of a love, jubilation, the zest for life closely linked to the desire for the living God. A childhood of the Church! Not at all a nostalgia for the Church of the early ages . . . Here as elsewhere, it is important to take present-day realities into account. And the Church on this earth is not made up of angels, but of very human beings with their shortcomings.

If we understand our own limitations, can we still reject the Church when its structures become an obstacle? That would mean that we know ourselves too little, and it would also imply a lack of love for those who in all honesty are working within those structures. Rather than being brought to a standstill, try to pass through the structures like the water of a brook which always manages to find an outlet . . . In spite of its frailties, a childhood of the Church will appear . . . and the freshness of a communion will spring up, a source of inexhaustible confidence.

Who would not wish to open a way of life for those they love rather than blocking the road? And for all who seek to love Christ, loving him also means "preparing the way." Who could love Christ and yet remain indifferent to the continuity of Christ in the ongoing history of humanity?

Where can we draw the courage to bring about reconciliation? A hopeful sign today: on the part of Christians, a growth of awareness concerning the most critical situations of the world community has never been more widespread.

And still more: nourished at the sources of contemplation and prayer, men and women are becoming capable of overturning the most dismal perspectives and finding the courage to take risks to bring about reconciliation and peace.

In their commitment to follow Christ, often those who try to change the structures of society make this discovery: in a technological world, inner laws can provoke a fissure between prayer and work. When struggle and contemplation are viewed as opposites, as if one had to be chosen to the exclusion of the other, that opposition ends up by tearing apart the very fibers of our being.

And that is true for us all: the core of our being finds its harmony when daily activity and prayer become one.

People Of Peace

THE ECUMENICAL VOCATION is assuredly ordeal by fire, a combat which requires complete self-mastery. In the face of tensions, only contemplative waiting allows us to preserve that inner vitality which comes from our love for Christ and for his Body, the Church. In order not to get bogged down in useless discussions or justifications which satisfy nobody, and above all to keep alive a vision of the needs of contemporary society, it is vital for our wills to be tempered in the wellsprings of contemplation.

No one who does not quench his thirst there can remain serene in the face of attitudes which must be analyzed if they are not to bring us to a dead halt in our progress, attitudes which otherwise may well sap our vital energies.

There are the pressures to conform in various ways, and the resistances to all the changes which unity will require. There are the Church leaders who call themselves ecumenists, yet keep postponing the day of visible communion so that, in fact, they exclude its possibility. There is also the small-mindedness of people, by no means uncultured, who seem to have an irresistible need to put labels on their neighbors, twisting the meaning of their words in an attempt to stifle all dialogue. There is incomprehensible jealousy, an open sore in the People of God. Jealousy seeks compensation by neutralizing the dynamism of new ventures.

Was it not Bernanos who wrote that all adventures of the spirit are a *via crucis?*

Every road to reconciliation involves a continual dying to self. None of those who travel this road can avoid trials and sufferings, even if they are sometimes tempted to run away from them.

To every Christian community God gives a place of peace and joy where we can rest in him alone, and pass through both trials and days of gladness. Conversing with God stimulates fervor. It sets us in the communion of all the saints, alive or departed. It prepares and nourishes our communication with others by making us reflect God as bearers of his peace.

When, with two of my brothers, I met Pope John XXIII for the last time, he explained to us how he came to his decisions in very simple prayer, in serenity, in conversation with God. "I have a dialogue with God," he said, adding immediately: "Oh! Very humbly. Oh! Quite simply."

When we converse with God, we do not expect any extraordinary illuminations. We know that the most important thing, for ourselves and for others, is peace. Anyone who listens, by day or through the long watches of the night, is given the answer: peace!

Inner peace! Not a peace uttered by the lips while within there is war. Not a peace acquired once and for all, for there is still the burden of our own self and the incompletely healed wounds in which all kinds of feelings are still festering—bitterness, the passions seething in our flesh, illusions of impossible love or the discontent of love disappointed. All this weighs us down and tears us apart, but the peace of Christ is able to reach into the depths, even into the deepest wounds of our being.

Peace is not inner passivity nor escape from our neighbor. The peace of Christ has nothing in common with that insipid tranquility in which the horizon contracts more and more, and in the end crushes the victim it encloses.

No peace is possible if we forget our neighbor. Every day the same question rings out: "What have you done with your brother?" A peace which does not lead to communication and communion is nothing but illusion. People at peace with themselves are led to their neighbor. They inspire reconciliation and peace among those who are divided.

The peace of Christ needs time to mature, for it must heal the wounds of trials and sufferings. But now they no longer overflow; they are kept within oneself, and their hidden presence releases vital energy.

By their inner harmony with God, people of peace are already an anticipation of unity. They carry others along with them.

A Passion To Forgive

WHERE WOULD WE be today, if women, men, and even children had not come forward at times when humanity seemed to be heading for the worst? They held on to a fine hope in humanity and to an invisible presence.

They found a way to go beyond personal conflicts and to cross the barriers which separate nations and people of different spiritual families or races. They perceived, rising up from the heart of the peoples of the earth, an aspiration to a fullness of joy and peace, but also an endless lamentation.

As for you, will you let yourself fall asleep in dull indifference? If you are dismayed by the mistrust that exists between nations and by the wounds left by broken human relationships, will you let your lips and your heart become frozen in a continual attitude of "What's the use, we can do nothing, let things take their course"? Will you let yourself sink into discouragement like Elijah, a believer of times gone by, who, seeing that he could do nothing more for his people, lay down under a tree to fall asleep and forget?

Or else will you remain awake?—You have a long journey ahead of you. Will you take your place among those women, men and children who have decided to act?

They possess unsuspected strengths. By their very simplicity, their lives speak to us. They foster sharing and solidarity and dispel the paralysis of indifference. They disarm mistrust and hatred. They are bearers of trust and reconciliation. Knowing that God does not wish armed conflicts or any other human suffering, they take action. By doing all they can to make the world a place fit to live in, by understanding with a trusting heart and living by forgiveness, they become creators with God.

If a passion to forgive became a burning flame within you, you would be kindling a spark of communion that reaches even the most tragic situations.

Do we not realize? God wants us to be creators with him. He has accepted a huge risk: he has wanted human beings not to be like passive robots, but free to decide on the direction their lives will take. He leaves us free to forgive, but free also to reject forgiveness; free to create with God or not.

There is no limit to the depths of the human being. These depths open toward the depths of God. And God is already there waiting for every person, deep within them. It is there that creative energy is born.

Can there be no miracles on earth?—Yet love which forgives is one. It opens a whole new space before you and you find yourself free, completely free. You sense within you something that is of God and which cannot ever wear out. The contemplation of God's forgiveness gives rise to a radiant goodness in the simple hearts of those who let themselves be guided by the Holy Spirit.

The Risen Christ who is invisibly present could speak in this way: "I know that you sometimes go through monotony and darkness. But I can tell you this: I am in you, beside you, and in front of you. 'Happy those who trust without having seen.' "

You doubt and say to yourself, "The fire in me is going out." But it was not you who lit the fire. It is not your faith which creates God, nor can your doubts banish him to nothingness.

Faith means trusting simply in God—a trust so simple that it is open to everyone.

If one's heart is attentive, trust in God makes it possible to manage with very little.

With this little, God brings about what really matters and everything is simplified in oneself, including one's way of living and way of approaching others.

Completely simple, too, and stripped of all pretensions remains your humble prayer of self-giving. And all through life, who is not surprised to find oneself saying to God, "Listen to my prayer, the prayer of a child"? Day after day, inner struggles continue. Struggle and contemplation come together.

You would like to feel the presence of God and instead you have the impression that he is absent. Do you realize that, wherever there is forgiving love, God's presence is almost tangible? Though your heart has difficulty believing it, his Spirit is continually active within you.

If you were to let a passion to forgive without delay burn within you, you would be setting out on a spiritual adventure, the wonder of a love. God loved you before ever you loved him. You think you do not wait for him, and yet he is waiting for you. You say, "I am not worthy," and he places on your finger a ring of celebration, the ring of the prodigal son. That is the transformation of the Gospel.

We are all prodigals! In the depths of your captivity, when you turn toward God, all humiliation disappears from your face. God's forgiveness becomes a song within you.

Giving yourself to Christ, trusting in him, forgiving others, is all one and the same life-giving movement.

When you seek to forgive, you will encounter resistances in yourself. Forgiveness does not come naturally to anyone, it is a pure reality of the Gospel. When you are shaken, hurt and humiliated, will you go on forgiving till your very last ounce of strength?

When you forgive and come up against a refusal, the answer of the Gospel is clear: it involves showing kindness without waiting to be understood, and forgiving in the face of distance and coldness, even to the point of giving up trying to know what the other person will do with your forgiveness.

Is your forgiveness being taken advantage of? The love which forgives is not blind; it bears the stamp of clearsightedness. Those who forgive are not shielded from suffering when others say to themselves, "I can do anything I like and even break this person—I know I'll be forgiven in the end anyway."

Forgiveness is a very personal step. It restores us to transparency of heart. Far from leading to a lack of concern for others, it awakens our attention to those who are oppressed, or mistreated, or manipulated. It frees the strength which is needed for an involvement with them.

When wounds of the past become reopened, will you find the courage to forgive even those who are no longer on earth?

Are you ready to love only those who love you? Anyone can do as much, and without needing the Gospel. Praying for those who hurt you counts for a lot.

During your inner struggles, God was present without your knowing.

As you advance without seeing, as if shrouded in darkness, what struggles you pass through! Striving, not so much against doubt, but to be found faithful and to dare to give yourself, right to the very end, in a yes for life.

Some think that only outstanding people are able to take on the commitment to such a yes. But every person, each with his or her humanity, can create a lifelong commitment in God.

For those who choose to follow Christ, a yes and a no sometimes wrestle within. Any choice means deciding from among various options, while it is natural to want to have everything and not give up anything.

Through the yes of faith, the yes of trust in God, the Risen Christ makes you fully alive, he wishes you upright, not swaying in one direction and then another. By remaining faithful, you express to God the absolute nature of your love.

In our inner struggle, none of us is abandoned to a desert of loneliness. From the time of his resurrection, by his Holy Spirit, Christ Jesus' mysterious presence takes form in a visible communion, the Church. Gathering women and men "from all peoples, he has made them mystically into his own Body." With this communion in the Body of Christ, God is offering you a foundation for the whole of your life.

Because of Christ and the Gospel, will you prepare yourself every morning to forgive? As you do, you will see a space of freedom opening out before you which no one can take away. From now on, seeking to create with God, will you go forward in simplicity with what you have already understood?

For trust to become a reality in the world, in the East or the West, in the North or the South, your life and the lives of a multitude will be needed. A lifelong experience is not necessary in order to begin, nor the understanding that comes with accumulated knowledge. How could you be at peace as long as you have not found where to rest your heart?

Witness To A Different Future

SOMETIMES YOU ASK me where is the source, where is the joy of hoping.

I will answer you.

All your past, even the moment that has just gone by, is already swallowed up, drowned with Christ in the water of your baptism.

Don't look back: that is part of a Christian's freedom. The important thing is running to meet what is to come.

Give up looking back. Not in order to be irresponsible. If you have wounded your neighbor, would you leave him lying on the roadside? Would you refuse reconciliation, refuse to pour oil on his wound?

Give up looking back. Not in order to forget the best of your past. It is up to you to celebrate the times when God passed through your life, to remember your inner liberations.

You will say that to forget the devastations of sin is impossible, no one can do that . . . tenacious, stabbing regrets remain.

If your imagination brings back destructive memories of the past, at least be aware that God, for his part, takes no account of them.

Have you understood? One of the greatest risks in living Christ for others is forgiveness. To forgive and to forgive again, that is what wipes out the past and plunges you into the present moment.

Christian, you bear the name of Christ: for you every moment can become fullness of life.

The word love is so often abused. Living out a love that forgives is another matter.

You can never forgive out of self-interest, to change the other person. That would be a miserable calculation which has nothing to do with the free gift of love. You can only forgive because of Christ.

You will dare to pray with Jesus his last prayer: "Father, forgive them:

they do not know what they are doing." And spontaneously this second prayer will arise: "Father, forgive me: so often I don't know what I am doing either."

Forgiving means even refusing to take into account what the other will do with your forgiveness.

Forgiving: there lies the secret stimulus that will make you, too, a witness to a different future.

Aflame With Christ's Love

IF WE ARE to keep our fire, in God's today, then the living charity of Christ must come to feed the flames with constantly renewed friendship for every human being, all our brothers and sisters.

It is not at all a question of betraying the truth; but we must stress the fact that there can be no truth without love. Relations between Christians today require love before anything else; once it is present, such love will lead us to refuse the all too easy and all too human attitudes by which we have learned to become judges of one another. If there is no conversion to the love of Jesus Christ, how can we ever hope to see profound changes in our denominational attitudes, which have taken shape over generations?

Part of our progress toward oneness will involve acquiring this firm hope: the Lord will surely bring us to communion, he has the power. Our task is simply not to rebel against the means he chooses to employ.

Already, many people are wondering in their heart of hearts whether they can hope for unity come what may. Yes, because that was Christ's last prayer: "May they all be one . . . so that the world will believe." This means that visible communion is not just a human aspiration; our faith demands it. It is not dictated by external circumstances; it is obedience to Christ.

The inner attitude corresponding to this new obedience will flow from a life lived intensely in Christ. Such a life does not foster sentimental nostalgia for unity; it is a virile force which will break down within ourselves all those forms of opposition to others which have been consuming so much of our vital energy.

Loving the Church. Loving her as Christ loved her, and accepting that she will always have to make her way across the deepworn ruts of her children's sinfulness—their spirit of division and self-righteousness. Loving the Church, in spite of the mediocrity of some of those who bear heavy responsibilities within it. Loving the Church, in the best as well as in the most compromised.

In this way the Church of Christ advances through time. It is alive to the extent that it is inspired by the love of all its faithful. It is strong when its members arm themselves, day after day, with the endless patience of faith. It is humble when its people, far from condemning with smug bitterness, are prepared to love it to the point of giving their lives, today and every day, in the attempt to renew it.

Any other road can only lead to the spirit of self-sufficiency and schism, while still not righting the wrongs condemned.

External judgments inevitably harden and imprison those who bear the brunt of them. We must admit that neither the steadfastness nor the excellent arguments of the Reformers who left their original confessions succeeded in reforming a Church whose transformation they longed for with all the hope of which they were capable. And that is not at all to underestimate the importance of the reforms they called for: they were necessary. But how can we who come after them hope for changes if the calls to renewal emanating from new forms of Christianity—so soon loaded down with layer upon layer of polemic and strife—are devoid of any love for the reality which lies hidden beneath even the most hidebound of traditions?

When our hearts are finally empty of all bitterness and open to be filled with infinite friendship toward every person we encounter, we shall find that people are able to accept our comments and our teaching. When the love of the living Christ grows within us, we find it impossible to burden others with a bad conscience. We become able to love even those who oppose us. And then a Christian can be sure of moving on firm ground, can be sure of being in God.

There is one example in history of an authentic reform: Saint Francis of Assisi. He suffered for the Church, loving it as Christ loves it. It would have been easy for him to pass harsh judgments on the institutions, the customs and the callous attitudes of some of his fellow Christians. But that is precisely what he refused to do. He chose instead to die to himself, waiting with burning patience until at last his love-filled waiting brought about renewal.

The Lord brought his People through the desert, and he has the patience to lead us still by his sovereign power. He is capable of raising up prophets from among his People.

Today, only Christ can kindle in us the fire of his love, to make us leaven in the dough. Some are called to express communion by their words, others receive the gift of fervent intercession, while others are asked to offer their lives, to make a gift of themselves which may demand a hard struggle, while the point of it all remains hidden. What matters is for each Christian, by means of these varied gifts, to become a ferment of communion in the Church.

The means at our disposal seem very slight. The yeast and the dough look so much alike that our lives strain to see the difference. Yet invisibly the yeast contains the power to transform everything. Everything is hidden within it, and therefore the infinite becomes possible.

Yeast must always be well mingled with the dough. And each of us must be present at the heart of the Church and of the world, with that discreet presence characteristic of every life hidden with Christ in God.

What we renew is liable to harden again one day, just as the outer layer of the dough hardens with age. And so it is up to us to prepare others who will be able to put in new leaven after us. This is how Christ's Church, and those who give it life, are renewed.

If our lives are offered in these varied ways, then, although we may not know how, consequences will arise from these modest beginnings, consequences which are incalculable.

One day, says the Apostle, the gift of tongues and the gift of prophecy will disappear, knowledge will cease, but love never passes away. We may perform heroic deeds, or have faith enough to move mountains, we may give everything we own to feed the poor, and even go so far as to give our bodies to the flames; yet, without love, it will all be in vain.

We may achieve marvels, but only those will really count which result from Christ's merciful love alive within us. In the evening of life we shall be judged on love, the love we allow gradually to grow and spread into merciful kindness toward every person alive, in the Church and throughout the entire world.

FOLLOWING YOU, O CHRIST
(Prayers)

O Christ,
tirelessly you seek out those who are looking
for you
and who think that you are far away;
teach us, at every moment,
to place our spirit in your hands.
While we are still looking for you,
already you have found us.
However poor our prayer,
you hear us far more than we can imagine or
believe.

Lord Christ,
at times we are like strangers on this earth,
disconcerted by all the violence and harsh
oppositions.
Like a gentle breeze,
you breathe upon us the Spirit of peace.
Transfigure the deserts of our doubts
and so prepare us to be bearers of
reconciliation
wherever you place us,
until a hope of peace arises in our world.

Open in us, O God, the gates of praise,
so that we can say with Christ:
"Father, into your hands I commend my spirit."
You know how poor and vulnerable we sometimes
are.
We thank you, Lord Christ, for our human frailty,
for it sets us on the road where,
by trusting in you,
we are made aware of the only thing that matters:
your life within us.

Jesus, Risen Lord,
you change and transfigure our heart just as
it is.
You do not even ask us to uproot the weeds;
you take care of that.
With our wounds, the thorns that hurt us, you
light a fire—and a way forward opens in us
to welcome your Spirit of compassion and the
Spirit of praise that brings healing.
So that what is most resistant in us, our
failures, our refusals and our inner abysses
may be transfigured into energies of love
and reconciliation, all you ask of us is that
we welcome you and rejoice in the miracle of
your forgiveness.

Lord Christ,
you take us with our hearts just as they are.
Why should we wait for our hearts to be changed
in order to go to you?
You change them, day by day,
without our knowing how.
You have all that is needed to heal us:
prayer, hymns, forgiveness,
and the springtime of reconciliations.

Agreeing to lose everything for you, O Christ,
in order to take hold of you,
as you have already taken hold of us,
means abandoning ourselves to the living God.
Centering our life on you, Christ Jesus,
means daring to choose:
leaving ourselves behind so as to no longer
walk on two roads at the same time:
saying no to all that keeps us from following
you, and yes to all that brings us closer to
you,
and through you, to those whom you entrust to us.

Christ Jesus, by your Spirit
you come and kindle a burning light in us.
We know well that we are not the ones
who create this source of light,
but you, the Risen Lord.
To all of us,
you give the one thing that matters
and which is hidden from our own eyes:
a peaceful trust in God
and also poverty in spirit,
so that with a great thirst for the realities
of God,
we may take the risk of letting you accompany us
O Christ,
and of accompanying, in our turn,
those whom you entrust to us.

O living God,
you no longer knew how to express to human
beings that you are nothing but love and
forgiveness,
that you never want suffering for anyone,
that you never punish.
And so, to make yourself understood,
you came to earth in poverty,
through your Christ.
Now risen from the dead,
Christ Jesus is present
by his Spirit in every person;
he is there for those who suffer trials.
As we advance with you,
one day we shall tell you:
Sing in me, O Christ,
your love has burnt into my soul.

Like your disciples on the road to Emmaus,
we are so often incapable of seeing that you,
O Christ, are our companion on the way.
But when our eyes are opened
we realize that you were speaking to us
even though perhaps we had forgotten you.
Then, the sign of our trust in you
is that, in our turn, we try to love
and forgive with you.
Independently of our doubts
or even of our faith,
you, O Christ, are always present:
your love burns in our heart of hearts.

Lord Christ,
even if we had enough faith to move mountains,
without love
what would we be?
But you love us.
Without your Spirit who dwells in our hearts,
what would we be?
But you love us.
Taking everything upon yourself,
you open for us a way toward the peace of God,
who wants neither suffering nor human distress.
Spirit of the Risen Christ,
Spirit of compassion,
Spirit of praise,
your love for each one of us
will never fail.

Risen Jesus,
you are there close beside each person,
you descend to where we are,
to the very lowest point of our human condition.
And you take upon yourself all that hurts us,
both in ourselves and in others.
You accompany every human being.
More than that,
you visit even those who, as nonbelievers,
have died without having been able to know you.
And so, in our inner struggle,
the contemplation of your forgiveness
gives rise to a radiant goodness
in the humble heart that allows itself to be
led by your Spirit.

Close to you, Christ Jesus,
it becomes possible to know the realities of God,
by letting the little we understand of the
Gospel pass into our daily life.
And this little proves to be just enough for us
to advance, day by day, moment by moment.
You never turn us into people who have made it,
but humble people of God who, in all simplicity,
are seeking to place their trust in you.
O Christ,
you take upon yourself all our burdens
so that, freed of all that weighs us down,
we can constantly begin anew
to walk with lightened step,
from worry toward trusting,
from the shadows toward the clear flowing
waters,
from our own will toward the vision of the
coming Kingdom.
And then we know,
though we had hardly dared hope so,
that you offer to make every human being
a reflection of your face.

Lord Christ,
for us to tell you: "Lord, I believe,
come and help my lack of faith,"
you open a path of creation.
And on this path, you enable us to create
even with our own frailty.
Praised be the Risen Christ, who, knowing us
to be poor and vulnerable,
comes to pray within us the hymn of an
unchanging confidence.

Following you, O Christ,
means passing time and time again
through the mystery of death and resurrection
—that Passover which remains incomprehensible
for our human condition.
Whenever we encounter you,
you ask us to leave ourselves behind and to follow you.
At those moments when,
if we are to love with you and not without you,
we must abandon some project contrary to your plan,
come Lord Christ,
so that we may realize that your love will
never disappear.
Come and fill us with the quiet assurance that
to follow you is to give our life.

You are the God of every human being
and, too bright for us to look upon,
you let yourself be seen as in a mirror
on the face of your Christ.
We are eager to glimpse a reflection of your presence
in the confusion of people and events:
open in us the gateway to transparency of heart.
In that place of solitude
which exists in each one of us,
come and refresh the dry and thirsty ground
of our body and our spirit.
Come and inundate us with your trust
till even our inner deserts burst into flower.

O God, Father of all the peoples of the earth,
by your Christ you reconcile everything to yourself,
to the point that nothing can ever be disastrous
except losing a spirit of forgiveness.
Lord Christ,
in your presence,
we are sometimes at a loss,
but you remain in us, and we in you.
Come, Spirit of the Risen Christ,
on those days
when reconciliation involves an inner trial.
Come and sing within us
and raise us up by the trust you have in us.

Lord Christ, enable us to place our trust in you
and so to live in the present moment.
So often we forget that you never want human suffering,
but peace in our hearts.
Christ Jesus,
by your Spirit you dwell in us.
Still more, you pray in us.
Your miracle within us
is accomplished
through the trust we have in you
and your continual forgiveness.

O Risen Christ,
you breathe your Holy Spirit upon us
like a gentle breeze
and you tell us: "Peace be yours."
Opening ourselves to your peace,
letting it penetrate
the harsh and rocky ground of our hearts,
means preparing ourselves to be bearers of
reconciliation wherever you may place us.
But you know that at times we are at a loss.
So come and lead us to wait in silence,
to let a ray of hope shine through in our world.

POSTFACE

PERSONALLY, I have always lived in the certainty that a small number of women and men, spread across the face of the earth and striving to reconcile in themselves struggle and contemplation, could change the course of history and reinvent the world, because they hoped against all hope.

BIBLIOGRAPHY

Books by Brother Roger of Taizé

Living Today For God (revised edition of *This Day Belongs to God*), London-Oxford: Mowbray and Minneapolis: Winston-Seabury.

A Life We Never Dared Hope For, Minneapolis: Winston-Seabury.

Afire with Love, New York: Crossroad.

Meditations on the Way of the Cross (with Mother Teresa of Calcutta), New York: The Pilgrim Press.

Parable of Community: Basic Texts of Taizé, London-Oxford: Mowbray.

Brother Roger's Complete Journal in Six Paperback Volumes, first published in English by Mowbray (London–Oxford).

Festival Without End (1969–70).

Struggle and Contemplation (1970–72).

A Life We Never Dared Hope For (1972–74).

The Wonder of a Love (1974–76).

And Your Deserts Shall Flower (1977–79).

A Heart That Trusts (1979–81).

Also Of Interest

The Story of Taizé by J. L. G. Balado, Minneapolis: Winston-Seabury.

A Universal Heart: The Life and Vision of Brother Roger of Taizé by Kathryn Spink, San Francisco: Harper & Row.

Other Resources

Taizé Video: 30-minute documentary entitled *Taizé: That Little Springtime,* Journey Communications, P.O. Box 131, Mt. Vernon, Va. 22121.

Music: Songbooks (Vocal, Instrumental, People Editions), Records and Tapes are produced by G.I.A. Publications, Chicago.

Letter from Taizé: Bimonthly newsletter, including daily Bible readings; yearly subscription in U.S. $6.00. Address:

Taizé Community
71250
Cluny, France

Tel.: (33) 85.50.14.14
Telex: COTAIZE 800753